HADLEE
ON CRICKET

HADLEE

ON CRICKET

The essentials of the game

RICHARD HADLEE

ANGUS & ROBERTSON PUBLISHERS

Angus & Robertson Publishers

First published in 1982 by A.H. & A.W. Reed Ltd, Wellington, New Zealand.
This edition first published in the United Kingdom by Angus & Robertson (UK) Ltd in 1983.

ISBN 0 207 14493 1

Typeset by Computype Services Ltd, Wellington, New Zealand
Printed by Kyodo-Shing Loong Printing Industries Pte Ltd, Singapore

Contents

Acknowledgements

A number of people helped me in the preparation of this book and I would like to take this opportunity to pass on to them my grateful thanks for all their help.

First to a number of friends and players who have very kindly allowed me to photograph them for the book: Geoff Howarth, Ian Smith, John Bracewell (all New Zealand), and Derek Randall (England). Thanks for your help.

The following photographers whose work appears in the book also deserve my thanks: Peter Bush, Rob Tucker, Martin Barriball (all New Zealand), and Patrick Eagar and John Sumpter (England).

Robin Craze of the New Zealand *Cricketer* magazine also provided much assistance, and Mark Raffety executed the line drawings.

Finally, Martin Horton, the New Zealand national coach, read the original manuscript and made a number of valuable suggestions which have been included in the book.

R. J. H.

This cricket coaching book is dedicated to all those parents, coaches and school teachers who give up their time to see that young cricketers enjoy the sport. It is my hope that this book will help them develop and improve their game by a greater understanding and appreciation of the finer points of what I believe to be the greatest game ever invented.

FOREWORD

Many sportsmen and women are blessed with what is called a natural aptitude for their particular sport, but very few of them reach the top by sheer natural ability alone. At some stage or another they have all had to learn the basics of the sports, practised those skills, and then blended skill with natural ability.

Richard Hadlee — or "Paddles", as he is nicknamed — is a cricket player of great ability and talent, but I am sure he would be the first to admit that even he would not have reached the heights he has without learning the basics of his art at a youngish age. (This does not mean that you *have* to be young to learn or improve your cricket, but for the fundamentals to become almost habitual it is perhaps better to learn young.)

I will always remember my own early cricketing days — at the age of eight or nine, being coached by my father. Now my Dad has hardly ever played cricket, but that did not stop him from showing me that if I was to be a batsman, I first had to learn to watch the ball, play straight, defend my wicket and not hit the ball in the air. Or if I was to be a bowler I had to bowl straight and on a length or I'd get hit all round the ground.

Dad spent hour after hour throwing a ball at me, repeating over and over again, "watch the ball", "play straight". Not having pads in those days, if I did not play straight I usually ended up with my stumps knocked over, or in considerable pain and sometimes tears after catching a hard ball on the legs. If I was bowling and I wasn't accurate I spent a lot of time retrieving the ball back from over the fence.

Now I didn't like getting sore shins or wasting time looking for balls that had been hit over the fence. Therefore what Dad was telling me was important and made sense. But no matter who the coach is, it is equally important for the pupil to persevere with what has been taught and to work extremely hard to achieve maximum potential.

It is *not* boring. The more one learns about cricket, its techniques and its art, the more one wants to know. As no one, in the history of cricket, has yet completely mastered the game, you can be assured of continual learning, as with life in general.

This book by Richard Hadlee is an invaluable guide to the cricketer of any age. Those who read it, learn by it and work hard at what Paddles is trying to convey will, I am sure, both improve their game and find it a great deal more enjoyable.

GEOFF HOWARTH

INTRODUCTION

"I have frequently been asked if I was born a cricketer. I do not think so, because I believe that cricketers are made by coaching and practice, that nerve, eyesight, physique and patience, although necessary, would not be much use alone."

W.G. Grace, 1899

This quote from one of the great legends of the game demonstrates that even he considered practice of the basic techniques of the game to be necessary to the successful player. I believe also that correct coaching and an understanding of the finer points of the game are necessary for consistent success, enjoyment and reward.

Public interest in cricket has greatly increased in recent years, to a large degree because of the different types of cricket played today. There are five-day test matches; three-day first-class matches; one-day and day-night matches; and indoor competitions. Television has brought some of the magic and character of the game to millions around the world. In addition there are now far more opportunities for players themselves. Attacking and cavalier batsmen can indulge themselves by playing one-day cricket, whereas the more technical and patient type of players will find their niche in five-day test matches. (Often, however, a blend of both kinds of players will be found playing in any game.)

The game itself still depends on the new incoming players, and the development of a young player depends greatly on the encouragement he or she gets from parents, schools, coaches and clubs.

I have been disturbed to notice a complete lack of interest in the game in some schools that I have visited. There are often no pitches, poor equipment (if any) and a lack of coaching knowledge in teachers. It is my hope that this book will stir interest in the game and provide an incentive to young players at school and club. Cricket is, after all, a game that caters for youngsters of different physical and mental make-up. It allows for individualism and flair without destroying team spirit. It rewards the trier as well as the gifted, and it teaches patience and fair play.

Cricket has allowed me to tour the world representing New Zealand, and I'm grateful for the life and livelihood it has given me. Many friendships both on and off the field, competition with and against some of the best players in the world — these are things I will treasure for the rest of my life.

CHAPTER ONE

Approach to the game

The attitude of the player

AIM OR GOAL

It is a natural instinct to have ambition, so why not in cricket? We all need something to strive for, so set yourself a goal, whether game by game or long-term. Whatever your target, try to achieve it. Whether you do so or not doesn't really matter. At least the *desire* to will give you a better chance of being successful. You may want to score 100 runs per game or take five wickets per game. You may want to represent your province or country. Try!

CONFIDENCE

Every cricketer should believe in his own ability. Confidence breeds success whereas lack of confidence is a passport to failure. You should back yourself in any given situation by rating your own ability. If you believe that the bowler can get you out then invariably he will do so. On the other hand, if you believe that he is not good enough to get you out then you have a better chance of survival.

I have played and watched a lot of cricket, and it disturbs me to see players and even a whole team talk themselves out of a good performance because conditions are not in their favour.

In losing the toss, a team can be placed at a disadvantage, but complaining about that along with bad pitches, and fearing the opposition's fast bowlers and best batsmen, won't help the situation any. No matter what conditions are like, you *must* adapt yourself quickly. Adjust your technique and have a positive approach.

OPPORTUNITIES

Everyone should make the most of opportunities that come their way. They are often few and far between, so one has to realise that "lucky break" and cash in, so to speak. If you are fortunate enough to be selected for a special coaching programme or an under-age representative side, then these are opportunities for you to develop and improve your game in front of possible selectors. It could influence your cricketing career.

I've always said that the greatest opportunity that came my way was when my brother Dayle accidentally caught his big toe in a lawn mower. He was unable to play in the remaining three first-class fixtures of that 1971–72 season. I was his replacement and was fortunate enough to capture some wickets including a hat-trick and was selected to play for a New Zealand "B" team in Australia that same season. From that point I've never looked back.

FITNESS

This will be dealt with under a separate chapter, but it is worth stating here that it is important to be fit prior to and during the game. No one can possibly perform to his best level if he carries an injury during the game or becomes tired and lacks concentration because he hasn't prepared himself well. Regular exercise such as jogging and sprinting and practice in the nets will prepare you for greater efficiency and performance in the face of fatigue or tiredness and will prevent or delay injury.

TRAINING AND PRACTICE

Stick to a regular and set programme. When

1

at the nets, practise correcting a certain fault until it has been mastered. Then correct something else. Don't waste time at the nets. It is better to practise particular facets of the game for an hour than to spend two hours messing about and not achieving anything specific.

LISTEN AND LEARN

Listen to what people have to say. Shared knowledge can help. It may be boring and frustrating sometimes, but someone may just mention an aspect of play that you haven't thought of and which could improve your game.

WATCHING GREAT PLAYERS

Your game can be greatly helped by attending international and provincial cricket matches at the local ground, and by watching great players in action, or on television, and reading books on the sport. Study techniques. Listen to sports commentators because they will pick up faults, correct them and explain why captains and players make various decisions.

You may even like to consider *thinking* like an admired player. Dennis Lillee has been one of the greatest influences on my bowling and sometimes when I've been bowling badly, I've said to myself "What would Lillee do in this situation?" More often than not, the solution has become apparent.

TEAM GAME

A team of 11 players, playing together with a common will and desire to win, should beat a group of individuals. Although each member in a cricket team has been selected for a particular job, and concentrates on that task, he also takes an interest in the game as it affects the other 10 players. Too many teams have the odd individual interested only in themselves — this can upset other players and the team as a whole. Once a team is picked, play together.

PLAY HARD AND TO WIN

Obviously we play the game to win. That

means you must compete hard, giving nothing away to the opposition. When in a winning position, never take it for granted that the game is won. The game isn't over until the last ball has been bowled.

Too often I have seen games lost from a winning position because the team has relaxed — even for only a short period of time — and their advantage has been lost. You have got to *make* things happen.

PRAISE AND ENCOURAGEMENT

A great individual and team motivation is the congratulation of fellow team-mates. If a player has taken a wicket, scored 100, dived and stopped a certain boundary in the field, or taken a brilliant catch, say "well done". Your appreciation could inspire him to bigger and even greater things.

SUPPORT THE CAPTAIN

The captain has been given the job of leading the team and making decisions. The selectors have faith in him to do just that. It is therefore important to support the captain and back his decisions. Of course he will sometimes make mistakes and decisions may backfire, but he needs your support. If you haven't got confidence in your captain it will affect your own game and bring the team to disarray.

ENJOYMENT

If you don't enjoy the game, then don't play it. Cricket is a great leveller, full of ups and downs, failures and successes. If you haven't got the temperament to handle certain game situations then you will not enjoy the game.

GOOD SPORTSMANSHIP

All sportsmen want to be successful, so they play the game hard. It is important to be competitive, but it is more important to play the game fairly and within the laws of the game. Accept decisions whether they be good or bad. When you lose, congratulate the winning team — you would expect the same if you had won.

Good sportsmanship is respected by other

All players need this kind of support from their team mates. Qadir of Pakistan gets complete support from his fieldsmen as Mike Gatting of England is given out lbw.

cricketers who will enjoy playing against you. If you have a reputation for being a bad sportsman then others will make the game unpleasant for you and the enjoyment of the game could disappear.

Recording personal statistics

If you are a real cricket enthusiast and have a "pride-in-performance" attitude, then you may like to record your own individual cricket performances, day by day or game by game. The following simplified chart will prove a useful score sheet.

Let's say you have five two-day games to be played. There is a maximum of 10 batting innings so a batting aim might be 300 runs averaging 30 runs per innings. There is a maximum of 10 innings to bowl in so your aim is 20 wickets at 20 runs per wicket.

3

Game opposition	Bowling					Batting	
	Overs	Mdns	Runs	Wkts	Average	Runs	How out
1 Team A	10	2	30	2	15.0	25	Caught at slip off seam bowler
	15	5	40	1	40.0	35	Caught mid-off — spinner
2 Team B	10	3	20	2	10.0	40	Caught keeper off seamer
	5	1	10	0	—	10	Lbw seamer
3 Team C	15	5	30	3	10.0	0	Run out
	15	4	40	1	40.0	60	Bowled seamer
4 Team D	10	2	20	1	20.0	30	Caught slip - seam bowler
	10	3	20	1	20.0	10	Caught keeper - seam bowler
5 Team E	20	5	60	6	10.0	20	Caught mid-off — seam bowler
	10	0	60	3	20.0	20	Lbw seamer
	120	30	330	20	16.5	250	25.0 average

By looking at the chart you can assess the following.

BOWLING

Ø The 20 wickets were achieved at a better strike rate than anticipated — i.e. 16.5 as against 20.0.

Ø 120 overs were bowled for 330 runs, therefore conceding 2.75 runs per over. Ideally, two runs per over would have been more satisfactory so an improvement in line and length is needed.

Ø When the last game was to be played, you had only 11 wickets, needing nine in the last game to achieve your aim. A determined effort was made and the 20 wickets won.

Ø In the last innings that you bowled in, you were conceding six runs per over — far too many. Obviously, that was a bad day with line and length suffering quite dramatically compared with other performances. A lack of rhythm and concentration could have been the reason, so some extra work in that area has to be done.

4

BATTING

- Ø 250 runs were scored at an average of 25.0. You didn't achieve your aim because of too many low scores: 0, 10, 10, 20, 20.
- Ø In the last game you needed to score 90 runs to reach 300, but you fell short by 50.
- Ø The reason for your downfall is through being caught out six times in 10 innings. Hitting the ball in the air to be caught in the outfield, or not getting behind the line of the ball and so edging the ball to slip or to the wicketkeeper, could reveal a lack of concentration or a faulty technique that has to be corrected.

Look like a cricketer

There is a saying "If you cannot be a cricketer, then look like one" and it is amazing the difference it makes. One starts to *feel* like a cricketer and this helps your game. Too many times I have seen youngsters playing in tracksuits or black shoes, with the wrong size bat, pad on only one leg and so on. Be neatly and correctly dressed at all times. Keep your gear clean and well maintained.

This section on player attitude can be summed up by the thought that "a quitter never wins and a winner never quits".

Remember these three words:

Dedication — to achieve your aim you must practise and work hard.

Concentration — always keep your eye on the ball when batting and fielding. When bowling, watch where you want to pitch the ball.

Tolerance — accept the bad days and make the most of the good ones.

For the coach

Any coach who wants to gain the respect of his team and get the best out of them must be well organised. He should have a plan for each training session as well as achievement targets.

- Ø Practice areas should be well laid out and not cluttered. Allow plenty of room for players to develop their skills especially in group coaching.
- Ø Player safety is important. In the nets, for example, ensure that numbers are kept to about maximum of four — three bowlers and a batsman. Don't allow bowling while a bowler is retrieving the ball from the net and has his back turned. When picking up the ball in the nets players should always *face* the batsman and walk *backwards* towards the bowler's wicket.

In addition, the effective coach:

- Ø Should be able to demonstrate skills efficiently and correctly.
- Ø Must be able to detect and then correct faults of all cricketers.
- Ø Must be flexible. Certain players will have more natural ability than others and there may therefore be differences in techniques.
- Ø Should stress enjoyment of the game.
- Ø Ensures everyone has the right equipment and *looks* like a cricketer.
- Ø Is familiar with the laws of the game.
- Ø Should speak clearly and not move on to another subject until each point is clearly understood.
- Ø Stresses game etiquette — sportsmanship and accepting decisions. Too many youngsters (and even some of today's "name" players) make a show of looking at the edge of their bat when given out lbw, trying to create the impression that they hit the ball. A batsman should face the umpire when any appeal has been made. Every cricketer owes the umpire that courtesy.

Concentration

It is very easy for the mind to wander during the day's play. The game may become boring if you're waiting for a possible declaration, or the batting side is dominating the game, or the game is destined for a draw. Or you may be thinking about something else other than cricket — that's when mistakes are made.

Loss of concentration may result in a batsman hitting the ball into the air and getting caught. A fielder may misfield and drop a catch, while a bowler may lose his line and length and let the bat take the initiative. A captain may make a bad decision.

Always keep your mind on the game. (Several of the following points will be covered in more detail in later chapters.)

Batting

∅ Train yourself to *watch* the ball in the bowler's hand as he starts his run-up. Watch the ball leave his hand and come onto the bat.

∅ Study the pitch to see how it is playing. If the ball is coming through low then make sure that you are playing off the front foot to avoid the lbw. If there are any pieces coming out of the pitch, pat them down with the bat.

∅ If you are the non-striker, watch to see how your partner is playing the bowling. You may be able to offer him advice or vice versa.

∅ Watch for subtle variations of pace and the use of the crease by the bowler.

∅ If you have some difficulty with a bowler, play him out rather than take risks. Don't try to hit yourself out of trouble.

∅ Look for possible field changes as the bowler walks back to his mark.

∅ Achieve your batting aim by batting for minor targets. In trying to score a 100 it may take four hours and in that time there will be a lunch break and a tea break. Bat for sessions: e.g., get off the mark, lunch, 50, tea, 100, stumps.

∅ Count the balls bowled during the over. It would be a bad error of judgement to get out on the last ball of an over. It would also be a bad lapse of concentration.

Bowling

∅ Watch the target area where you want the ball to pitch.

∅ If you cannot get the batsman out try to bowl a maiden. Be mean. Begrudge giving away runs off your bowling.

∅ Be aware of your field placements and bowl to the field. Look to make changes if necessary.

∅ Watch the batsman's technique for possible weaknesses. Talk to the keeper about these weaknesses and about the proper line and length to bowl.

∅ Decide on the ball you are going to bowl and don't change your mind as you run up. This could result in a bad ball.

∅ If you are having a bad day or if you are being out-bowled by a fellow team-mate, let that make you more determined to bowl better and try harder.

Fielding

∅ Try to help the bowler get wickets and prevent runs by being alert and thinking that the ball is coming your way every time. Aim to save 10 runs in the field. If everyone did that, then there would be 100 less to score when it was your turn to bat.

∅ Watch the batsman's feet. From their placement you'll know whether he's likely to hit the ball on the off or leg side.

Ø Watch the captain for possible field alterations.

When there is a scoreboard at the ground, all players should make use of it in analysing the game's situation. A batsman can quickly assess the scoring rate needed per over to win the game. Conversely, the bowler and fielders will be aware that the batting side needs, say, four runs per over and will be trying to prevent that happening.

Always "think cricket". Be involved in what is happening.

Team spirit is an essential factor in a side's success. The New Zealand team is certainly showing it here at Wellington's Basin Reserve as an Indian batsman heads for the pavillion after having been dismissed by Lance Cairns (being congratulated by skipper Geoff Howarth at left).

CHAPTER TWO

The importance of fitness

Any sportsman wanting to perform to the best of his or her ability and to be a consistent and reliable performer must be physically and mentally fit. Otherwise the player will tire, letting himself and the team down.

The unfit or weary batsman may play a rash shot or he may slow down when running between wickets. The bowler may tend to bowl loosely, with full tosses or long hops, and may lose direction after 10–12 overs. (A bowler may have to bowl 20 overs in the day.) The wicketkeeper may miss a vital stumping or catch towards the end of the day's play.

Lack of fitness may also cause injury problems, which will prevent you playing at your peak.

Fitness programmes should be designed to help your particular facet of the game. Batsmen, bowlers, fielders and wicketkeepers will sometimes tackle different exercises to develop particular skills.

Training requires personal motivation. You must *want* to train. If you don't, you are conditioning yourself to failure. If you don't want to train, it will be easy to quit and say you've done enough for the day — when in fact you may have completed only half of the required workload.

General points

Ø Make training your own responsibility. Set aside time to do the work required and do it, even if you have to train by yourself.

Ø Training must be progressive. You cannot get fit in a few days and you cannot do maximums unless you build up your workload. For example, 20 push-ups may be your present maximum but you may have to increase this to 50 if you are bowling within, say, three weeks.

Ø While weight training is valuable cricketers should use light weights. Dumb-bells are sufficient. Seek advice and supervision on any increased lifting; many young bowlers, in particular, use weights to develop muscles and once finished find they become muscle-bound and very unco-ordinated. Weights tighten the muscles, so stretching exercises are necessary to keep the muscles supple.

Ø Warm up before batting, bowling and fielding — a light run and stretching exercises to loosen up the body.

Ø Don't neglect injuries. Get medical advice as soon as they occur and get them treated properly.

Ø Drink plenty of fluids, especially in hot climates. The body needs to replace all the perspiration it loses. Fruit drinks are good, but not fizzy drinks because the gas can cause stomach cramps. Don't drink too quickly. It may be advisable to add salt or sugar to your drink to prevent cramp. Don't drink too much alcohol at nights before a game.

Ø Watch your weight.

Ø Most cricket teams should have a good medical kit available for the treatment of injuries.

Bowler

The following programme is to be done in your own time. It is a guideline only. If you cannot do the required maximums, do what you can and increase repetitions gradually until maximums are achieved.

In fast and medium pace bowling, each ball involves the bowler in a quick sprint to the crease of anything up to 20 metres — and then a rapid rotation of the hip and back as the arms do a complete circle. There is strain on the groin, the front leg and the ankles and it is vital that bowlers prepare for this strain in their fitness programme.

Endurance running and sprint work will build up the necessary stamina. Once you've achieved a basic fitness try 5 kilometres a day initially, building up to 8 kilometres, plus 20 sets of 20-metre sprints per day for, say, four days a week. Running through parks and gardens is very refreshing and enjoyable and you'll find it the best time to analyse and plan.

The following exercises strengthen different muscles.

Alternate arm and leg raises for the back — Lie on your stomach raising your right leg and left arm. Repeat with the left leg and right arm and do this 20 times each side.

Double back-lifts — Lie on stomach with hands on your buttocks. Lift chest and legs off the ground and repeat 20 times.

Press-ups for the shoulders and arms — Body weight is on the arms and toes. Push body up and down. Bend arms until body is horizontal and straighten until elbows lock. You should be able to do a minimum of 40 in two minutes.

Sit-ups for the stomach — Lie on back with arms behind head and sit up until your legs are in a bent position with your feet firmly on the ground. A minimum of 60 to be done in two minutes.

Side back muscles — Lie on back with feet off the ground and knees in a bent position. Shoulders are pinned to the ground while both legs move to the left side with the knees touching the ground and then to the right side, 20 sets to be done. Also, stand in upright position and push sideways down the left side as far

Back arch, method one.

Back arch, method two.

Back arch, method three.

9

Strengthening the back.

Press-ups.

Sit-ups.

as you can go and then the opposite side. Do this for two minutes.

Hamstring exercises — Stand in upright position. Cross legs over and bend as far down as possible and hold for five seconds. Repeat 10 times on each leg. Find a fence waist high, place one leg straight out on fence, and push down with the hands while bending forward to touch your head to the knee. Repeat for other leg.

Groin exercise — Spread legs apart and push down on one leg, stretching the groin. Repeat with the other side and do for two minutes each leg.

Ankle — Rotate ankle around so that it is very mobile.

Neck — Rotate, around and up and down, for two minutes.

Arms — Rotate backwards and forwards and then in alternate directions for two minutes.

With all exercises, don't bounce. Perform with timing and co-ordination.

Wicketkeeper

This player may walk as far as 6 kilometres during a day's play, as well as squat and rise up to 600 times, and jump left and right and trot 20 metres 200 times. So it is important that he does sprints like bowlers, plus a little running for endurance. Three kilometres per day is sufficient.

Individual exercises include:

Squats — Stand and squat doing three sets of 30 with gradual build-up in speed. Jog 15 seconds between sets. Do the sets with hands in front of body for the first set, hands on head for the second set and hands on hips for the third.

Thigh stretches — These prevent the thighs from hardening. Sit back with buttocks on heels and hold ankles with hands while both knees are on the ground and legs splayed. Stretch body back as far as possible. Repeat 10 times, building up slowly each session to get back as far as possible.

Side jumps — Adopt a squat position, with knees slightly bent. Jump from right to left and back again, 20 times each day.

Batsman

Time at the crease will involve much pivoting and sprinting. Exercise by sprinting as for a bowler, with some endurance running: 5 kilometres a day at your own pace for approximately 30–40 minutes.

Individual exercises include:

Squats

Lunging knee bends — Go well forward on one leg until back knee touches the ground. Do 20 on each leg, stretching as far forward as possible.

Knee tucks — Jump and tuck knees to chest 20 times.

Push-ups — four sets of 10.

Sit-ups — 20 repeats.

Rotation toe touching — Standing in an upright position with arms outstretched, swing around to touch alternate toes. Do 20 times each side.

Spring backs — With feet together, jump forward a metre and then spring back. 20 times each way.

Leg and arm crosses — Sit upright, legs well apart and have arms outstretched. Swing right arm to touch left toe and then swing left arm to touch right toe. Do 20 sets.

Springs — 20-metre bursts at three-quarter pace with quick turn at end of 20 metres and walk back. Repeat six times and build up to four doubles: i.e., 2 x 20 metre sprints then walk, repeated four times followed by 3 x 20 metre sprints and walk, repeated six times.

Team programme

All of the above should be done in your own time to prepare yourself prior to playing the

Side and hip muscles.

Stretching the side muscles.

Hamstring exercise, method one.

Hamstring exercise, method two.

Groin stretches.

game. When you arrive for team training, the programme may vary considerably. A typical team programme might include:

Ø   Jogging around the boundary — say, six laps (3.5 kilometres) in 15 minutes maximum.

Ø   Series of 50-metre sprints — say, six sets.

Ø   Circuit training: If in a gym, 10 players will be performing 10 different exercises to maximum level while the other member is running six lengths of the gym. When the runner has completed his lengths everyone moves around to a new activity until everyone has completed the circuit.

Exercises will include:

Running six lengths of the gym — maximum pace.

Press-ups.

Sit-ups.

Pull-ups — Using high bar, pull body off ground with head passing over bar and repeat.

Climbing up a rope.

Double back-lifts.

Climbing up wall bars — down and up again.

Lunge thrusts.

Tuck jumps.

Jumping up onto a bench and back onto the floor again.

Burpees — Squat with hands on the floor. Push legs back, squat and stand.

All exercises are repeated as many times as possible. Keep count of repetitions done on each exercise and next time at circuit training try to better them.

DUMB-BELL EXERCISE — Don't use weights that are too heavy: 4.5 kg dumb-bells are sufficient.

Push-ups — Stand in upright position with a dumb-bell in each hand and push arms up alternately, 20–40 punches each arm.

Sideways bends — Standing in same position, do sideways bend holding one dumb-bell. Bend as far as possible, 5–10 times each side.

Hip and arm rotation.

Thigh stretches.

Hip rotation and arm movement.

Sit-ups — Hold dumb-bell behind neck with both hands, and with feet wedged under something to prevent their moving do 15–30 sit-ups.

Alternate curls — With one weight in each hand bend one arm up to shoulder and lift the other high backwards. Rhythmical timing, 20–40 times.

Slow arm circles — Hold a weight in each hand and circle in both directions, 5–10 each way.

Arms raise and back arch — Lie face down on a bench with a weight in each hand. With dumb-bells on the floor, arch and raise forward, 10–20 times.

Upward jump — Squat with dumb-bell in each hand and jump upwards and back into crouch position, 20–30 times.

Shoulder shrug — Holding dumb-bell in each hand, lift and drop shoulders, 20–40 times.

Forward bend — Keep back straight, don't drop arms, and with dumb-bell in each hand and feet apart, bend knees slightly forward then stand up straight again. Repeat 6–10 times.

Deep lunge — With dumb-bell in each hand, raise weight above head and lunge the body forward over one leg. Drop arms to waist and raise again, lunging on opposite leg, 10–12 times.

Burpees.

Squats.

Pullover — Lie on back on bench with arms over end of bench. Holding a dumb-bell in each hand, lift slowly up and over and return, 10–12 times.

All the above should improve your fitness, alertness and reflexes, and make you a better

Knee tucks.

Rotation toe touching.

the injury is attended to, the sooner you'll regain fitness.

Common mistakes in training

⊘ Insufficient dedication — maximum effort is never achieved.

⊘ Too much emphasis placed on weights.

⊘ Training programme is not planned and some parts of the body are neglected, causing injury.

⊘ Diet is neglected — too much food and excessive drinking will nullify any training that you have done.

⊘ Training is not progressive.

⊘ Proper warm-ups prior to the game starting are neglected — players become susceptible to injury.

⊘ Injuries are neglected, and take longer to come right.

⊘ No medical kit available to treat injuries.

player. You won't get fit playing the game; you must be fit prior to the event. As well, maintaining fitness will aid you in avoiding injuries because your body will be in top form and you will enjoy the game a lot more.

If you receive a knock, pull a muscle or suspect a bone fracture, it is important you seek immediate medical advice. The sooner

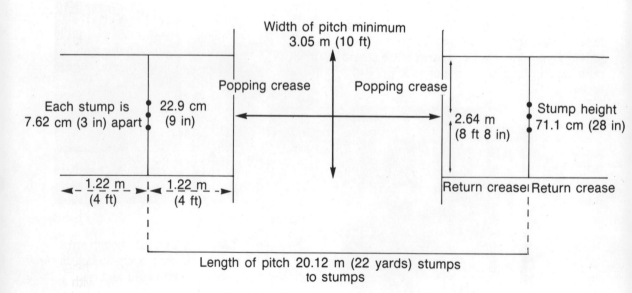

The dimensions of a cricket pitch

CHAPTER THREE

BATTING

The approach to batting

The accomplished batsman has good ball sense. He has the ability to pick up the line and length of the ball quickly and deal with it effectively. Skill in the latter area will involve good timing so that the ball is stroked effortlessly rather than whacked. Batting does not require brute strength. Bert Sutcliffe, one of New Zealand's greatest batsmen, was neither a big nor a strong man, yet with his exquisite timing and judgement he could hit the ball firmly to the boundary — as well as over.

An even temperament is also advisable. Play every ball on its merits rather than on what you *think* it should be. This means not getting carried away after hitting a four and trying to do the same to the next ball wherever it may pitch. The batsman on 44 or 94 who tries to hit a six to get his 50 or 100 regardless of the pitch of the ball throws away all the hard work of the innings so far and gives the bowler and fieldsman a chance of getting him out. (Obviously, if it's the right ball, then by all means hit it for six.)

Play one ball at a time. Concentrate on the ball bowled and determine not to get out — to play defensively to a good-length ball and to score runs from a bad ball. Once that ball has been bowled and played efficiently, forget it and switch your concentration to the next ball. A careless or rash stroke could end your innings and any chance of victory to your side. A batsman can usually make only one mistake.

Every batsman must realise that he bats for the team, not himself. The captain should give his batsman definite instructions on how to play the type of innings required to help the team take the initiative. It may be that a batsman has only 30 minutes to bat and the captain wants 30 runs. It is the batsman's duty to try to score the runs required — he should not end up 5 not out.

"Cricket sense" in a batsman is deciding what tactics to use in any given situation and against any given bowler. A batsman has to decide whether it is best to play defensively or attacking, and how to beat a particular field setting or overcome a difficult batting pitch. A lot of this will come with experience.

Early in his innings the batsman should play within the "V". He should hit the ball straight between mid-off and mid-on. If he starts hitting across the line (say, sweeping a spinner to square leg) before he has judged the pitch conditions and worked out what the bowler is actually doing, he is likely to sky it into the air to be out caught — or miss it completely to get out lbw or bowled. Play as straight as possible until your confidence allows you to play other shots 100 per cent correctly.

Taking guard

The batsman arriving at the wicket needs to know where he is positioned in relation to his stumps so that he can best sight the ball. The usual guard position has the batsman's head in line with the middle stump and his eyes level, but the placement of his bat may vary from middle stump depending on his height or his style of playing. A tall batsman with an upright stance may prefer to bat on middle stump or take two legs (i.e., middle and leg stump). A batsman who tends to lean over in

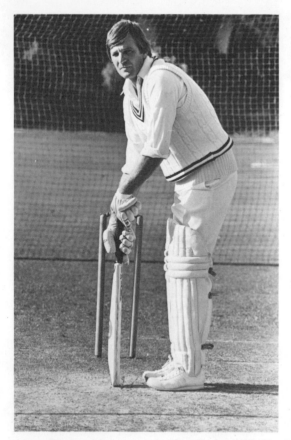 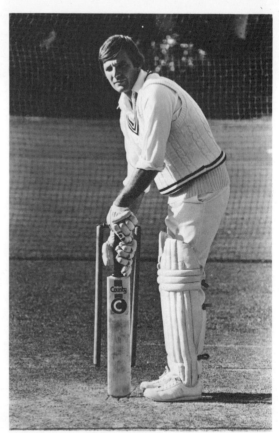

New Zealand test captain Geoff Howarth illustrates the two styles of taking guard — middle stump, and two legs or middle and leg.

his stance may take leg stump because his head and eyes are still over the middle wicket.

The guard taken may depend upon the type of bowler and the pitch conditions. For example, a right-hand batsman facing against an outswing/leg cutter bowler should bat on middle stump. This will put him in a better position to judge the ball — even letting it go outside the off stump. By batting on leg stump, the same batsman might not judge the line of the ball as well and play a little too freely, with the possibility of catches behind the wicket.

In asking the umpire for the guard, hold the bat in an upright position. For the middle guard, the face of the bat points towards the square leg umpire. In taking the two leg or middle and leg guard, the face of the bat shows to the umpire at the bowler's end.

Once the correct guard has been obtained, mark it on the batting crease with the edge of your bat or a boot spike, then position your feet on that mark. Generally, the umpire will give the batsman guard from directly behind the middle stump at the bowler's end as that is the line from which lbw decisions are judged.

The grip

Correct grip is vital because both hands have to work together to ensure control and power in playing shots on both sides of the wicket.

To help you get the feel of the right grip, lie the bat face down on the ground in front of you with your legs apart. Pick the bat up as if you were picking up an axe. That is the

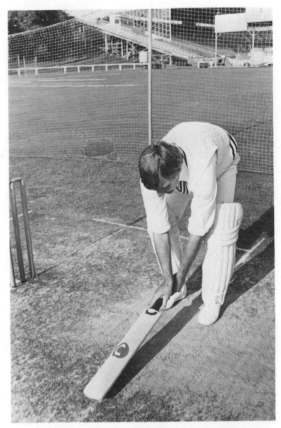

To achieve the right grip lie the bat down in front of you as shown.

Pick the bat up as if picking up an axe.

grip for batting. The hands are as close together as possible on the bat handle and just over halfway up the handle.

The top hand should grip the bat very firmly while the bottom hand grips loosely. Fingers and thumbs lie well around the handle and "V"'s are formed with the top and bottom hands. The first finger and thumb of the top hand are directly over the corresponding "V" of the bottom hand. The line of these "V"'s is between the splice and outer edge of the bat.

The top hand of the bat is allowed to rest against the thigh of the front leg. The top hand should point in the direction of mid-off and extra cover.

The front elbow is slightly bent.

Common faults in gripping the bat

⊘ The hands too far apart with the bottom hand too low on the bat handle. This prevents both hands working together in all straight bat strokes and allows the bottom hand to take control of the bat. A frequent result is that the ball is hit in the air.

⊘ The back of the top hand too far round and behind the handle. Again, this will restrict the stroke.

⊘ Both faults can be caused by using too big or too heavy a bat.

17

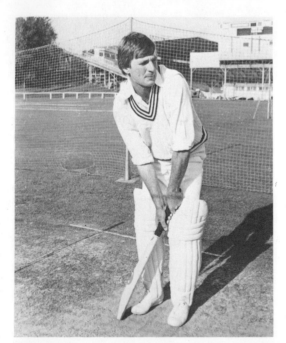

The correct grip and stance. Geoff Howarth's hands are together on the bat, his feet 15-20 centimetres apart. The knees are slightly bent, the body weight on the front foot, front elbow slightly bent, the head tucked into the shoulder, the bat tucked into the toe of the back foot.

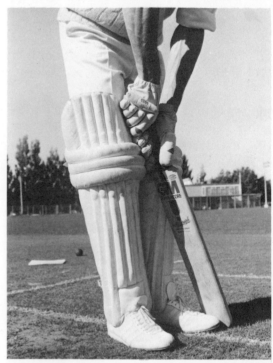

Although I am a right-handed bowler I bat left-handed. Here I illustrate the left-hander's stance.

The left-hander's grip. The top hand grips the bat firmly, the bottom hand loosely.

The stance

The stance should be relaxed and the batsman positioned so that he can best pick up the line and type of ball and play it.

The body — sideways with the head looking over the front shoulder towards the bowler.

The head — straight and still with the eyes level. The head should not be allowed to bob up and down when playing at the ball because by keeping his head straight and still the batsman can best sight the ball and judge how to play it.

The feet — a comfortable distance apart either side of the batting crease: i.e., 75–150 mm apart. The body weight must be evenly spread between the feet — never on the heels because this will restrict movement. The back foot should be parallel to the batting crease while the front foot can be parallel or slightly opened, pointing towards cover. The knees are slightly bent and relaxed to help quick movement. There should be no movement of the feet until the length of the ball has been judged, and then there should be a definite step back or forward — not both.

The bat — most batsmen prefer to have the toe of the bat grounded behind the back foot with the face of the bat pointing towards the pads and the hands resting on the front thigh.

An incorrect stance. Geoff's body is leaning over far too much, making it difficult to move the feet quickly into a playing position. The hands are too close to the bottom of the bat and the head is at an angle, poorly positioned to pick up the line of the ball.

Common faults with the stance

- Ø The feet too far apart, preventing quick initial movement.
- Ø The stance too open. This will lead to a crooked backlift and will make it difficult to lead with the shoulder into strokes on the off side.
- Ø The head badly positioned and not facing down the wicket. With the head held on an angle the eyes are not level and it is difficult to focus on the ball. Again, the head may not be in line with the stumps. Or if it is too far over to the off side it may cause the batsman to lose his balance.

Incorrect grip. The hands are too far apart on the handle.

Another incorrect grip. The hands are too far down the handle, and the finger should not be pointing down the back of the bat.

The backlift

To give the batsman the best chance of hitting the ball straight, the bat must be picked up straight and directly behind. Both hands are used in picking up the bat, the top hand dominating. The front elbow bends and the wrist "cocks", so that the face of the bat opens up and points towards point.

At the top of the backlift the front-hand wrist will be almost level with the front arm elbow. The bottom-hand wrist will be higher than the front elbow and the bottom elbow will also be bent.

Control of the top hand is vital. Both hands should be pushed back. This will ensure that the front shoulder is still pointing towards the bowler.

Against faster bowlers, the backlift will have to be picked up a lot sooner than against the slow bowlers, in order to give the batsman more time to play his shot. But be careful of the yorker, which may not give you time enough to bring the bat down.

The backlift. Geoff's bat is picked up shoulder high directly behind the back foot.

The left-hander's backlift.

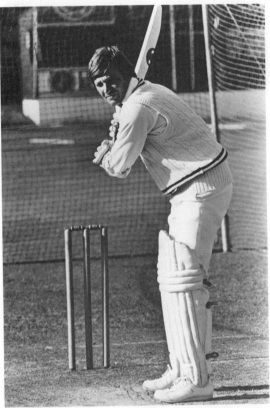

In the second the bat is picked up too wide.

Incorrect backlifts. In the first the bat has been brought back too far over the shoulder.

Common faults with the backlift

∅ The bottom hand taking too much control.

∅ The bottom-hand elbow being higher than the wrist, so that the face of the bat cannot open.

∅ Picking the bat up too late and having to hurry the shot.

Defensive strokes

This type of shot is played to a good-length ball, off either the back or front foot. The ball can be played just in front of or behind the batsman and generally no runs are scored from it. The ball is treated with respect.

FORWARD DEFENCE

This is played to a good-length ball. Playing straight in forward defence relies on the positioning of the front foot and the direction in which the head and the front shoulder move out to meet the line of the ball.

The batsman leads out to the line of the ball with the front shoulder and with the eyes watching the ball onto the face of the bat. His front foot will automatically follow in the same direction towards the ball and his body holds its balance as a result. The eyes must watch the ball onto the face of the bat.

The line of the shoulders must point parallel to that of the intended stroke. The wider to the off the intended stroke, the more the back of the shoulder should point to the bowler. For shots aimed at wide of mid-on, the shoulder and hip should lead in that direction. The body

Forward defence. Geoff's bat and pad are close together, his foot positioned to the line of the ball, his body weight on the front foot, his head directly over the line of the ball, his front elbow bent.

Australia's John Dyson illustrates the forward defence shot. He has moved his front foot well forward to the pitch of the ball.

Left-hander's forward defence. As the front shoulder points towards the ball the top hand controls the bat so that the ball is played into the ground. The back foot has eased up onto the toe.

must not fall away from the stroke or the bat will be pulled across the line of the ball.

The front foot must move out towards the pitch of the ball and just inside the line of the ball. The closer the foot gets to the ball, the less chance of it deviating off the pitch and going through any gap between bat and pad. The front knee is well bent to allow the body weight to come forward. The head should now be positioned over the front leg and in line with the ball. For straight balls the front toe should point down the pitch. If the ball is wide of the off stump, the toe will point to the direction of cover. If the ball is on the leg side, the front foot will have moved more to mid-on because the head and shoulder have moved into the line of the ball.

The heel of the back foot will automatically ease upwards as the body weight is moved onto the front foot.

The top hand controls the bat at all times. At the point of contact, the top hand is well ahead of the bottom hand so that the ball is hit into the ground. The bottom hand will ease itself into a slightly new position in which the thumb and the first two fingers dominate the bottom hand. (If the bat is continued to be gripped in the palm, it is impossible to play a forward defensive stroke correctly and straight.)

Common faults with the forward defence shot

- Ø Not leading with the head and front shoulder towards the ball.
- Ø Not taking the front foot far enough forward to meet the pitch of the ball. The batsman may lose balance and may actually fall over.
- Ø Not bending the front knee, leaving the batsman standing too upright. The batsman is then likely to let his bottom hand take too much control, and his head will lift into the air instead of facing the ball.
- Ø The full face of the bat does not meet the ball on contact.

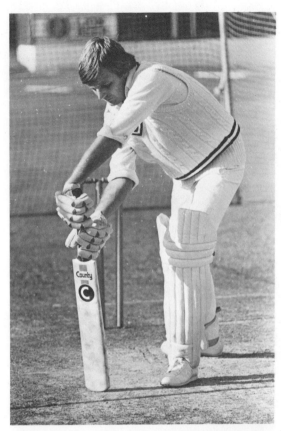

Incorrect forward defence. There is a big gap between bat and pad; the ball could easily go through it. The front elbow is too straight and the head is not over the line of the ball.

- Ø The top hand does not take control of the bat.

BACKWARD DEFENCE

This shot is played to a ball that has pitched short of a length.

The back foot moves back and just inside the line of the ball with the shoulder still pointing towards the bowler. The foot will land firmly and flat. To a straight ball, the foot should land parallel to the batting crease. If the ball is outside the off stump and the stroke is aimed at, say, mid-off, the toes will point backwards of the crease. For a ball pitching on leg stump, the back foot will open up and

23

Backward defence. Geoff's back foot has moved back and across. His head and the handle of the bat are in the line of the ball.

Left-hander's backward defence. The body weight is on the back foot and the front foot has eased up onto the toe. The front elbow is bent and very high.

turn towards extra cover, but the hips will turn to the leg side towards mid-on. The front foot follows the back foot to a natural position, eased up onto the toes and pointing towards extra cover.

The body and head should still keep their forward poise even though the body weight is now on the back leg. At the moment of contact with the ball, the head is kept well down, the back leg well braced and the eyes directly above and behind the line of the ball.

The front arm has control of the bat and the stroke. The elbow is very high and bent on contact with the ball. The thumb and the finger of the bottom hand grip the bat.

The full face of the bat will meet the ball,

the hands slightly in advance of the blade at contact. Again there is no follow-through.

Common faults with the backward defence shot

Ø Not stepping far enough back with the back foot, and not moving far enough over to get close to the line of the ball.

Ø Not picking the bat up high enough in the backlift to allow the ball to be played down.

Ø Not keeping sideways to the line of the stroke.

Ø Not keeping the head and balance of the

24

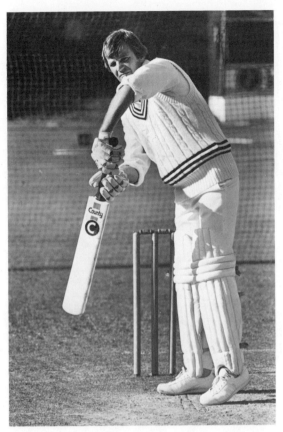

Incorrect backward defence. The back foot has not gone back and across to the line of the ball with the result that the bat has played away from the body.

body forward when making contact with the ball.

∅ Not controlling the bat with the top hand so that the ball is hit down into the ground.

∅ Not allowing the bottom hand to relax into the thumb and finger grip.

∅ Not keeping the front elbow high at the point of contact.

Attacking strokes

These shots can be played in any direction and are scoring shots. They can be played off the front foot or the back foot and include (assuming you are a right-hand batsman):

The straight drive — hitting back past the bowler.

The off drive — hitting the ball to the right and past the bowler.

The on drive — hitting the ball past and to the left of the bowler.

The cover drive — hitting the ball in front of the batting crease on the off.

The square cut — hitting the ball behind or just in front of the batting crease on the off side.

The late cut — hitting the ball very fine through the slips area.

The leg glance — hitting the ball fine on the leg side, behind square leg.

The hook — hitting the ball usually in the air behind square leg.

The pull — hitting the ball off the back foot, usually between square leg and mid-wicket.

The sweep — the ball is hit behind square on the leg side along the ground.

THE STRAIGHT DRIVE

This shot is played off the front foot to a ball that is over-pitched on middle stump. The ball will be stroked between the bowler and mid-off or mid-on. It is an extension of the forward defensive shot but with the bat following through. The front arm is kept as close as possible to the body to make sure that the blade of the bat is on line with the ball when contact is made. The bottom hand is also close to the body as the bat starts its down-swing after the pick-up.

Contact with the ball is made as close to the front foot as possible. The body weight is over the front foot and the body and eyes are well over the top of the ball. As the ball is hit, the arms have been thrown out in the intended line of the stroke.

Some batsmen will attempt to *loft* the ball

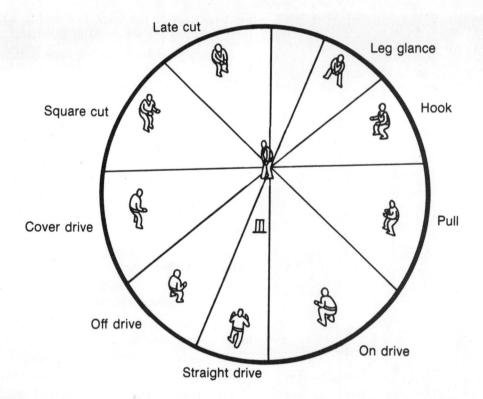

The range of attacking strokes.

over the top of the inner field when making this shot. In this case the bat meets the ball a little earlier, in front of the front foot. The body has been allowed to come up slightly as the bat reaches the hitting area. Both arms have followed through the intended line of the hit and there has been good arm extension.

THE ON DRIVE

As in all front-foot attacking strokes, the head and the shoulder lead towards the ball, into the line of the delivery. The front shoulder dips slightly and the front foot opens up towards the mid-on position. (A lot of top class players, however, will hit *across* their front foot straight down the pitch, or their foot will point towards mid-off.)

As the bat is brought down towards the intended direction of the shot, the front shoulder has moved away sooner than in other drives, in order to assist the direction of the intended stroke. Even though the ball is being driven wide of mid-on, it is important that the face of the bat is kept as square to the line of the stroke as possible.

At the point of contact, the arms are thrown away from the body. The top hand is still in control; otherwise the batsman may hit across the line of the ball.

At the completion of the on drive there is a full follow-through, shoulder high. The body is well balanced because of good front foot placement and the body weight is on the front leg. The back foot has eased itself onto the toe so that the body does not fall away to the off side.

The on drive. Although Geoff is driving to the on side he keeps the face of the bat as square as possible. The head stays down to help control the shot.

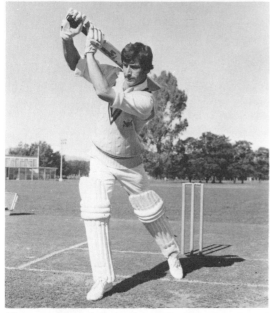

The on drive follow-through. The head and eyes are following the direction of the intended shot.

England's Geoff Boycott has moved beautifully into position to on drive, his body leaning forward and well balanced to hit the ball on the on side.

The cover drive and the off drive are really a continuation of the forward defence shot. Geoff Howarth's head is down throughout the shot.

THE OFF DRIVE, COVER DRIVE

This shot is attempted to an over-pitched ball on or outside the off stump.

The head leads out in the direction of the ball and the shoulder turns to face the ball. The front foot points towards the ball, making sure that the foot gets as close to the pitch of the ball as possible.

The body weight has transferred onto the front leg, which is bent at the knee. The top hand is firmly in control. Having the front shoulder pointing at the ball helps add power to the shot and allows the bat to travel through the line of the ball.

Contact with the ball is made close to the front foot. The bottom arm is close to the body and the hands are thrown out in the direction of the ball. The back heel is eased onto the toe and the front foot is firmly planted on the ground to help balance the body and is *not* allowed to pivot.

The follow-through is a continuation of the stroke after contact has been made with the ball and continues through the line of the ball. The head stays down at all times. The bat comes down quickly from the backlift and follows through.

This is one of the best shots in the game. Timing is vitally important if the ball is not to be hit in the air.

The follow-through. After contact with the ball the bat follows through and over the shoulder.

The shots of Greg Chappell on these pages were taken as he scored a majestic 176 against New Zealand in the Third Test at Lancaster Park, Christchurch, in March 1982. Here he illustrates the off drive perfectly. He has moved his front foot out to the ball by taking a big step forward, leaning his head and shoulder forward so that the ball is hit along the ground. After contact he follows through and is ready to run. Throughout the sequence his head has stayed down.

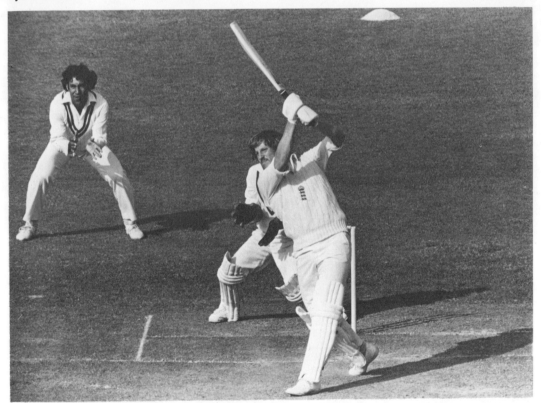

Ian Botham of England hits a four through the covers as he moves down the wicket to drive. His greatest attribute is his strength and his superb timing. Note the strong follow-through and the position of the batsman's head.

Australian keeper Rod Marsh watches as I drive the ball through the covers. The front foot is pointing in the direction of the shot and the head has stayed down in the follow-through.

Greg Chappell has driven the ball so late that his cover drive has become a square drive. Instead of hitting the ball through the covers he has noticed a gap in the field forward of point and delayed his shot. The square drive is played to a ball full in length and wide of the off stump. But it is a difficult shot to play and should be attempted only when the batsman has been playing for some time and when the pitch has a predictable bounce.

Geoff Boycott drives through the covers. He has stroked the ball with the body leaning forward so that the ball is hit along the ground. Boycott has scored 100 first-class centuries in his career.

Common faults with all the drives

Ø Poor backlift, the bat not picked up high enough. A short backlift will affect the timing of the shot and possibly hurry the stroke.

Ø Not leading with the head and the shoulder into the line of the ball.

Ø When driving along the ground, the front foot has not landed close enough to where the ball has pitched and as a result the batsman ends up playing away from his body, leaving a gap between bat and pad.

Ø The top hand is not controlling the bat. The bottom hand does the work instead, causing the bat to hit across the line of the ball.

Ø Not staying down when attempting the stroke, i.e. the head comes up in the air, the body loses its balance and the ball is hit in the air or missed completely.

31

○ Allowing the back foot to pivot, with resultant loss of body balance.
○ Not allowing the arc of the bat swing to be long and smooth and flat. The face of the bat should travel down the line of the ball for as long a time as possible.
○ Trying to hit the ball too hard.

THE STRAIGHT, ON, OFF AND COVER DRIVES PLAYED OFF THE BACK FOOT

This type of shot is played off the back foot to a ball that is pitched short of a length.

The back leg is well braced and the back foot moves back and across towards the line of the ball. As the ball makes contact with the bat, the front foot has eased itself onto the toes and the body weight is slightly forward. The head is behind the ball and the front elbow is held very high.

The body must be side on to the ball with the head down and forward.

The face of the bat will be open at the time of contact, with the top hand controlling. The power in the shot comes from the hands accelerating and the wrists uncocking just before impact with the ball. Don't try to hit the ball too hard or you may lose balance, rhythm and a lot of the power. The end result will be a mis-hit.

The back foot moves back and across in front of the stumps.

India's captain Sunil Gavaskar forces the ball off the back foot through the covers. Note the way in which his head has stayed down.

Attacking on the off side off the back foot. As with the backward defence shot the back foot moves back and across towards the line of the ball. At contact the front elbow is held high and the head is behind the line of the ball.

Greg Chappell's head stays down as he goes back and hits the ball through cover, following through with the shot. His body weight is on the back foot as he plays the shot, but he quickly moves it forward to take a possible run.

THE SQUARE CUT

This shot is played to a ball that is short of a length and wide of the off stump. The backlift must be high.

As the line of the ball is seen, there is a pronounced turning of the front shoulder. The back foot moves back and across the wicket towards off stump. The body weight is transferred onto the back leg.

From the high backlift every effort must be made to hit down on the ball. At the point of contact the arms are at a full stretch distance away from the body. As the ball is struck, the blade of the bat is slightly lower than the handle so that the ball is hit into the ground behind point and not in the air into the slips or gully positions.

The body weight must remain on the back foot while the ball is being struck.

The bottom hand rolls over the top hand to keep the ball on the ground.

Geoff Howarth illustrates the square cut. Note the way the bottom hand rolls over the top hand to keep the ball down.

Australia's Alan Border has initially moved his front foot forward but has then realised that the ball is short and a little wide of the off stump. He has started to bring his front leg back as he cuts the ball behind point. Although he has played the shot with no back foot movement he has executed it well because he has hit down and over the ball to keep it on the ground.

Geoff Howarth late cuts. With the body weight on the back foot the ball is hit down and fine behind point.

THE LATE CUT

This is basically the same shot as the square cut except that it is more delicately played with the ball hit very fine through the slips area. (The square cut is hit with a deal more force and the ball invariably goes to the boundary for four.)

Common faults with the cut

- Ø Not having a high backlift.
- Ø Not stepping across with the back foot, or not stepping far enough across to execute the shot correctly.
- Ø Not coming down on the ball at the moment of contact.
- Ø The body weight not on the back foot.
- Ø Not allowing the bottom hand to climb over the top hand.

Late cut by the left-hander.

Leg glance off the front foot. Geoff's front foot lands inside the line of the ball. His bat meets the ball in front of his pad, his bottom hand rolling the bat over the ball to deflect it down to fine leg.

Bruce Edgar, New Zealand opening batsman, leg glances a ball that has pitched on his leg stump.

THE LEG GLANCE (OFF THE FRONT FOOT)

This shot should not be played to a straight ball because there is little margin of error. It should be attempted only to a ball pitching on the leg stump and going further down leg. The ball will be fully pitched or on a good length, allowing it to be played off the front foot.

As with the other forward shots, the head and the shoulder will lead towards the line of the ball, with the body weight on the front foot.

The front foot lands inside the line of the ball, so that if the ball is missed it will hit the outside of the front pad. The hands are kept in front of the blade to ensure that the ball is glanced downwards.

To allow the batsman full control over the ball he must meet the ball in front of his front pad and directly under his head. The wrists are allowed to turn the blade of the bat slightly.

At the completion of the stroke, the body is not allowed to fall away, but is kept in advance of the front pad.

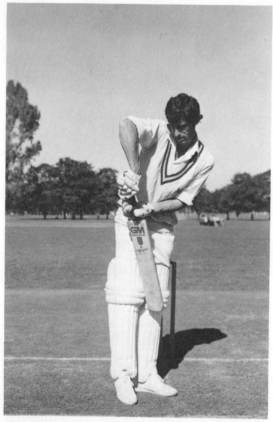

The left-hander's leg glance. As the ball is deflected to leg the wrists roll over the bat handle to keep the ball on the ground.

THE LEG GLANCE
(OFF THE BACK FOOT)

This shot is played to a ball that has pitched short of a length and is going down the leg side.

The back foot moves back towards the stumps with the body being kept slightly forward. The front foot moves back just inside the batting crease, opens up and points towards cover. It is positioned inside the line of the delivery.

The bat has been brought down close to the body with the front elbow very high. The top hand keeps the bat straight up and down, until contact when the handle of the bat moves slightly in front of the blade. Start to close the face of the bat at contact so that the ball is deflected behind square leg.

The ball must be allowed to come right up to the batsman. Wait for the ball to arrive, or the shot will be played too soon with the ball hitting the edge of the bat and offering a simple close-in catch.

Common faults with the glance

Ø Not placing the feet correctly. They must be placed inside the line of the ball and not outside the line.

Ø Not allowing the ball to come to the bat.

Ø Not keeping the head and the top of the bat over the ball at the point of contact.

Leg glance off the back foot. At the point of contact with the ball Geoff starts to close the face of the bat to deflect the ball behind square leg. The front elbow is held very high and the bat is brought down very close to the body.

The hook shot. Geoff's back foot has moved across the crease to the off side to give him room to play the shot. In his follow-through he pivots round in a half circle.

THE HOOK SHOT

This shot is played to a ball that is very short and arrives at the batsman chest high.

The batsman must move his weight onto the back foot very quickly. The backlift is made very early and is as high as possible. Sometimes the batsman has to rush his shot because the ball comes onto him very quickly or bounces higher than anticipated.

The back foot moves across the crease so that the foot is on the off side of the line of flight. The batsman sometimes goes back as far as possible to allow plenty of time to play the shot.

If he decides to let the ball go and play no shot he can let it pass over his head or shoulder by swaying away from the ball or ducking under it.

The batman's head is on the off side of the line with the ball, looking over his front shoulder.

The back foot pivots at the time of execution so that the bat and the body have moved around in a half circle. The batsman ends up facing nearly at the wicketkeeper. Always try to hook down — fast bowlers use this type of delivery and often put a fielder in a catching position for the shot near or on the boundary.

Common faults in hooking

- Ø Attempting to hook a ball that is too high.
- Ø Mishitting the ball too far in the air to a fielder.
- Ø Back foot does not pivot at contact.
- Ø Taking eye off the ball and turning the head or the back to the ball.

A young-looking Greg Chappell deals severely with a short ball outside the leg stump by hooking it fine. He has allowed his back leg to pivot and turn while his front (left) leg has been pulled right round towards the stumps.

The left-hander's pull shot. There is a high backlift and the wrists roll over the bat handle to keep the ball down.

The pull shot. The front leg is pulled around to outside the leg stump and the bat is brought down and across the body at full arms' length. At the point of contact the head is behind the line of the ball.

THE PULL SHOT

This shot should be played to a ball that is pitched well short of a length.

Using a high backlift the batsman takes his rear foot well back towards the stumps. The further and earlier it moves, the longer the batsman will have to watch the ball and have more control over the shot.

To enable the body to reach a completely open-chested position, the front leg has been carried away to the on side, the head remaining to the off side of the line of the ball. Both feet are now pointing almost down the pitch and both knees are slightly bent to ensure that the body weight is kept forward.

A combination of wrists and arms has brought the bat down and across the body to meet the ball at full arms' stretch.

The bottom hand has been allowed to dominate. It shuts the face of the bat as the ball is met. This will allow the batsman to hit the ball into the ground. The shot should be directed towards mid-wicket.

Common faults with the pull shot

- Ø Not taking the back foot back and to the off of the line of delivery.
- Ø Not carrying the front leg away to the on side to open the body square to the bowler.
- Ø Not ensuring that the head is directly in line with the ball and that it does not turn away after the completion of the stroke.
- Ø Not bringing the bat down and across the body from a high backlift.
- Ø Not striking the ball as near to full arms' stretch as possible.
- Ø Hitting late and aiming too fine.
- Ø The body weight not finishing over the back foot.

The sweep shot. When the bat hits the ball it is held at full arms' length and is horizontal. The ball is struck down, the wrists closing the face of the bat slightly.

THE SWEEP SHOT

This shot is played to a ball pitched on or outside the leg stump and spinning further down the leg side. The stroke is normally attempted by a right-hand batsman against an off-spinner, or by a left-hand batsman against a leg-spin bowler. On a very good batting pitch medium-pace bowlers can be swept.

The front leg lands in line with the ball. Upon landing, the leg bends, bringing the trunk of the body into a slightly forward position.

The head is held straight and the eyes are level. The bat has been picked up straight and the face of the bat is open.

The bat must get out to the line of the ball very quickly, being brought down across the body to make contact at full arms' stretch. At the point of contact with the ball, the bat must be horizontal.

The head has not moved its position and the eyes are firmly focused on the ball. The back leg has collapsed and the knee is on the ground.

To ensure the ball is struck down, the bat has been kept on top of the line of flight and the wrists allowed to close the face of the bat slightly.

Common faults with the sweep

- Ø Not leading with the head and shoulder on to the line of the ball.
- Ø Not landing the front foot in line with the ball and not bending the knees. If the knees are not bent, the body is too high and the execution of the shot is far harder.
- Ø Not making contact with the ball at full arms' stretch.
- Ø Not coming down on the ball, and instead hitting the ball in the air.
- Ø Not keeping the head still at the moment of contact and immediately after the shot has been played.

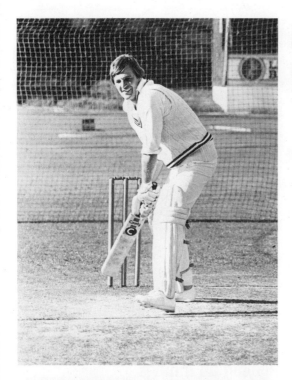
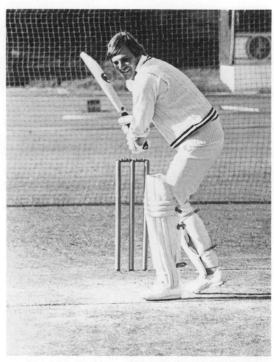
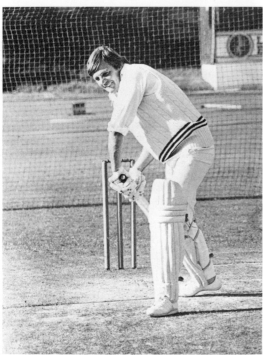

Geoff moves down the pitch to drive. This is one of cricket's great shots and is usually played with a flourish. The batsman uses his feet to advance to the pitch of the ball, which is driven straight or through the off side.

The left-hander moves out to drive. I have moved out to the pitch of the ball by crossing the back leg behind the front. The front leg leads into the ball with the body weight on the front foot.

MOVING DOWN THE PITCH TO DRIVE

This usually occurs when a slow bowler is bowling and the batsman has time to advance down the pitch to turn a good-length ball into a half volley or a full toss.

The front foot moves down the pitch with the back foot moving directly behind it, thus keeping the body side-on to the ball and ensuring that the head and shoulder lead into the stroke. If the ball has pitched outside the off stump, the batsman's back has almost turned on the bowler as he hits the ball through the cover field. His front hip will be close to the line of the intended stroke. The arc of the bat swing is kept very low and flat. As the bat comes down to meet the ball, the bottom hand is powerfully reinforcing the top hand without itself controlling the bat nor shutting the face of the bat on impact.

After the shot has been played, the batsman's body weight is firmly balanced on his bent front leg with his head still leading. The face of the bat has been allowed to swing down through the line in an extended and accelerated arc.

Playing an innings

The object of this section is to examine in detail a batsman's approach to his innings, to understand the planning of his play.

Let's assume that our batsman has practised hard, has a good technique and can play attacking shots. He is number five in the batting order. One of the opening batsmen has got out, so he goes into the changing room to put his pads on. He gives himself plenty of time to do this, because if he is rushed he will not be in the right frame of mind to bat.

Now he is padded up with his gloves and bat close by.

He moves out of the changing room and into the sun to adjust to the light. Remaining in the dressing room where it is dark will make it difficult for the eyes to focus quickly when it's his turn to go on.

Sitting as close as possible behind the wicket he watches the bowling carefully to analyse what the bowler is doing with the ball and to see how the pitch is playing. This provides some ideas on playing the conditions before he is actually out there. This is a big advantage. For example, he may notice that a medium-pace bowler is bowling outswingers at one end while an off-spinner at the other end is flighting the ball well and turning it quite sharply. Straight away he knows to let the swing ball go through outside the off stump, and that he must get well forward to the spin bowler to "kill" the spin.

Studying the field placements will help our batsman discover what the bowler is trying to do. Two slips and two gullys will suggest that the bowler is an outswinger or bowls a leg-cutter, and will be attacking off stump. If there are five fielders on the leg side then the bowler is attacking the leg stump. The batsman notices that the fielder at cover is very fast at moving into the ball and cutting off any short singles so there is no chance of taking a run there. However, the fielder at third man has a weak throw, so the batsman could take a run as he throws the ball into the keeper.

Another wicket goes — two down, and our batsman is next in. Instead of worrying, he sits down next to the latest out batsman and asks him questions about how the pitch is playing and what the bowlers are doing with the ball. The batsman just out may give him good advice. The pitch may be slow and low and the advice is to push forward on the front foot. Moving back and across with a low ball may expose the batsman to an lbw or bowled decision.

Numbers one and four batsmen are still at the crease and runs are flowing steadily with neither batsman in any difficulty. This certainly gives the number five batsman more confidence. But then number one gets run out by the cover fielder who has threatened on several occasions (our man has already noticed that).

Now he is in. He walks briskly to the wicket, passing the incoming batsman on the field of play. He is constantly reminding himself to play every ball on its merits and get into line behind the ball.

Our batsman takes guard and has a quick glance around the field to see where the field is set. He then settles down to take strike against an outswing bowler.

The first two balls are outside of the off stump. Our man lunges forward and misses both deliveries. Instead of being upset, he realises that he must let the ball go next time it is outside the stumps. Next ball he receives a fast straight delivery that he has to clamp down on. It reminds him that he must pick his bat up earlier to give himself more time to play his shot. At the conclusion of the over, he watches his partner play out an over from a left-arm spinner and notices that the ball is turning away quite sharply from the batsman. He now knows that if the ball pitches on middle, he will have to play the ball as if it had pitched on off stump. He positions his bat there so that the ball spins onto the face of the bat.

Our batsman has been in 15 minutes and has failed to get off the mark. This has not bothered him greatly because he can see that the field is well set and the bowling has been accurate. There is a gap in the field, however, and he waits for the right ball to come along. It does, and he hits it into the gap. He has now broken his duck, his innings has started and he is satisfied that he is more relaxed and finds batting a little easier.

Both batsmen have a talk at the end of the over. It is only 10 minutes to lunch and they agree that they must still be there then. Both agree and lunch duly arrives.

During lunch both batsmen can reflect on the morning's play. The captain may issue them new instructions.

After lunch both batsmen settle down to start their innings again, building on their scores and playing cautiously.

Four overs have been bowled after lunch and our batsman sees that his partner is having trouble with the left-arm spinner. At the end of the over, the two batsmen have a discussion and agree to a plan that will see our man facing the spinner and his partner the seam bowler at the other end.

Eventually number five's partner gets out. The incoming batsman is a big hitter and hits the first ball for four behind square leg. However, he does not notice that a fielder has been placed there for the next ball. Number five very quickly tells him of the field alteration and suggests to his partner that he should settle down and give him the strike because he is the in-form batsman.

As the wickets start to fall, number five becomes conscious that the tail order is long and that there is not a great deal of run potential left. With this in mind, he starts to force the scoring rate along, with perhaps the odd calculated risk taken.

The last batsman is at the crease and plays and misses at the first two balls. At the end of the over number five goes down the wicket to give him advice and encouragement. The batsmen agree to take short singles and to give our man the strike whenever possible. The fast bowler becomes frustrated with the singles taken so he bounces the ball at number five — it is a long hop and is hooked for four.

Our man has now reached 50 and he has hardly played a shot. He hears the applause and is well satisfied with his performance but his job is not yet done. He must not lose concentration because now he should have his sights on 100.

The fast bowler has been removed from the crease and is replaced by the left-arm spinner bowling to number 11. The field has surrounded him in close catching positions. He pushes forward, which is dangerous, but he survives the over. Number five takes strike to the left armer several overs later and decides to move the close-in catchers away from the catching position by attempting to sweep against the spin. He does so successfully, a dangerous shot to play but a calculated risk at this stage of the innings.

Runs have come steadily and the last wicket yields a further 50 runs. The captain declares at 250/9. Our man is congratulated by his team for scoring 75 not out. The innings has boosted his confidence and his team's morale.

Batting against different types of bowlers and on various pitches

PLAYING THE BOUNCER

The bouncer will pitch short of a length, the bowler intending it to rise sharply and quickly onto the batsman's chest and head. It is bowled at extreme pace and is used to unsettle the batsman. Because the bouncer can make the batsman feel very uneasy the bowler hopes that he will play a rash shot and get out (usually by miscueing the ball and hitting it behind square on the leg side).

Whichever way a batsman plays this delivery, he must pick up the line and length very quickly and move into position.

∅ He can duck under the ball and safely let it go over his head.

∅ He can stand up and sway away from the ball as it goes past his eyes, or sway forward and let it go behind his head.

∅ He can hook if the ball is no higher than head-high. If you are not a good hooker this shot should not be played. A miscue means that the ball will go in the air and you may get caught off the glove or the bat. If the ball is over your head let it go to the keeper. There is little chance of controlling a hook shot with the ball at that height.

However you play a bouncer, never take your eye off the ball. Never duck your head nor turn your body or back on the ball. Always follow it until it has gone past you.

PLAYING AN OUTSWINGER/ LEG-CUTTER

This type of delivery will leave the batsman either in the air or off the seam towards the slips.

∅ A good-length ball pitching on middle stump and hitting off stump should be played defensively off the front foot and

Two ways of playing a bouncer. If the ball is very short you can duck under it and allow it to pass over your head. Always keep your eyes on the ball – and keep the bat down.

Or you can sway either inside or outside the line of the ball. Remember to keep your eyes on the ball.

hit back to the bowler or to the mid-off field. Make sure that your front foot is inside the line with the pitch of the ball.

Ø A short-of-length ball bowled straight will not swing, but it could seam. Move onto the back foot and play the ball to the off or leg side in the "V": i.e., between mid-off and mid-on.

Ø A ball full outside the off stump can be driven through the cover field or to mid-off. If the ball starts to move away in the air, let it go. If it is pitched down leg, turn the ball to fine leg or hit to mid-wicket. There should not be much movement in the air or off the seam.

Ø A short and wide ball can be cut or pulled/ hooked.

PLAYING AN INSWINGER/ OFF-CUTTER

Ø A good-length ball pitching on off stump and hitting middle should be played defensively off the front foot, the batsman making sure that pad and bat are close together, leaving no gap for the ball to pass through. Do not pad up to this ball; because it is moving in towards the batsman he can be out lbw if he offers no shot. The ball should be played as straight as possible. Do not attempt to drive because the ball may move too much and your positioning may not be quite right.

Ø A ball pitched short of a length outside off stump and moving onto leg can be played off the back foot and forced into the on

47

field. The body will open up towards the on side and the batsman will hit the ball with the seam off the pitch or with the direction of the swing. Don't cut.

Ø A ball drifting down and outside the leg stump whether full or short of a length can be deflected down to fine leg or picked up and swung over and behind square leg.

Ø A full ball pitched outside off stump can be driven straight — but watch the swing. The further up the ball is pitched, the more it is likely to swing.

Ø A long hop should be pulled in front of square on the leg side for four or six.

PLAYING AGAINST A TURNING BALL

(a) AN OFF-SPINNER

Ø A good-length ball pitching outside off stump and turning to hit the stumps. Make sure that your wicket is protected at all times by pushing forward. Make contact with the ball with your bat and front pad close together, leaving no gap for the ball to go between. If you don't, the ball could go through the "gate" and hit the stumps. The top hand of the bat controls the bat so that the face of the bat is pointing downwards and the ball is hit into the ground. The bottom hand must not be allowed to push the bat in front of the pad or the face of the bat will be pointing upwards and the ball will go in the air.

Ø An over-pitched ball outside the off stump is played differently. Don't drive the ball too wide of the off stump through the covers because if the foot is not fully to the pitch of the delivery the ball may pitch and turn sharply and go through the "gate". It would be safer to drive as straight as possible.

Ø A short-of-length delivery pitched wide and short and turning back should not be cut. You may get an inside edge off the bat and the ball may deflect onto the wickets.

It would be safer to play off the back foot and force the ball between mid-off and extra cover. If the ball is a little straighter and short, get onto the back foot and defend the ball by playing defensively and hitting the ball back to the bowler or to the leg side. The ball may turn down the leg side, so allow the body to open up slightly and hit the ball with the spin to the leg side.

Ø A long hop from an off-spinner should be punished, the ball being hit to leg with the pull shot towards mid-wicket and square leg.

(b) A LEG-SPINNER

Ø A good-length ball pitching on middle stump and hitting off stump should be played defensively by pushing forward to "kill" the spin. If you cannot quite reach the pitch of the ball to kill the spin play at the ball as if the ball had pitched on off stump and wait for the ball to turn onto the face of the bat.

Ø An overpitched ball on or outside off stump can be driven through the covers. When driving make sure that the body is leaning well forward to keep the ball on the ground, the head well over the ball. If the batsman leans back, the head will go upwards, the bottom hand will control the bat and the ball will be hit in the air.

Ø A short-of-length delivery pitching on the stumps should be played defensively and hit into the off side towards cover to mid-off. A short ball outside the off stump can be cut behind point because the batsman is hitting with the spin.

Ø A long hop can be pulled or cut, preferably cut or whacked through the covers off the back foot.

BATTING ON A WET OR DAMP PITCH

On this sort of pitch the ball will come through very slowly and it will be difficult to play attacking strokes, especially driving. Short balls can be pulled easily enough or cut, but good-length balls will have to be played very carefully. These are difficult conditions to bat in, so it will take longer than normal to score runs if the bowling is tight.

There will be an attacking field with close catchers around the bat; the covers, mid-off and mid-on will be closer to the bat to prevent singles.

Best methods of scoring are pushing the ball and deflecting it fine, keeping it on the ground. Very bad balls can be hit over the top, but your timing must be perfect.

BATTING ON A FAST, BOUNCY PITCH

Most fast bowlers will try to get a lot of bounce out of these pitches, so they will tend to bowl short of a length. You must therefore be prepared to play off the back foot — but watch for the ball that is pitched fuller, tempting you to drive. You may see the ball further up and play at it too soon before your body is positioned correctly. Do not be in too much of a hurry to smash it through the covers for four.

The field set will be attacking with slips and gullys because the ball is likely to fly off the bat into that area or lob into a close catcher off the glove. Cuts, drives, pulls, pushes and deflections are the best methods of scoring.

BATTING ON A GOOD BATTING PITCH

The ball will bounce consistently, making it possible for you to play attacking shots to balls pitched on a good length or even just short of it. A batsman should relish these conditions because the bowlers' effectiveness has been nullified. Big runs should be scored here. Front and back foot shots all around the wicket can be played freely once a batsman has established himself at the crease.

In these ideal conditions too many batsmen start hitting boundaries at the start of their innings. They get a brilliant 30 or 40 runs because the batting is so easy, but then they get out. The field set will be very defensive, the fieldsmen placed in run-saving positions.

BATTING ON A LOW, SLOW PITCH

The ball will come through to the batsman very low and often slowly. The batsman must look to push forward on the front foot and not get caught halfway (that is, neither going back nor forward).

Many batsmen get out lbw on these pitches because there is no bounce. It is difficult to play forcing shots, so pushing the ball into gaps and deflecting it fine are the best methods of scoring. It will be difficult to hit the ball over the field and driving will be difficult. Play safely and surely until confidence allows you to do something different.

BATTING ON UNPREDICTABLE PITCHES

These are the hardest conditions to play on, essentially because the batsman doesn't know what the ball is going to do. The ball may pitch on the same spot twice but do two completely different things. It doesn't help the batsman's confidence, and it enables the bowler to bowl a consistent line and length, letting the pitch do the work. It is very easy to say that the batsman must still get in behind the line of the ball, even if it jumps disconcertingly off a length and hits him in the body.

In these conditions only guts and determination will allow you to survive and score runs. If you are afraid of the ball or the pitch it will be only a matter of minutes before you are watching the game from the dressing room. Looking for marks on the pitch may also not help your confidence.

You should simply play each ball on its merits and not give your wicket away by playing a rash shot. The field set will be semi-attacking because the captain will want to save runs as well as get the batsman out.

Batting problems

Batting is not always easy, even if the basic fundamentals are being observed. There are a number of factors that can upset a batsman's style of play, but most can be corrected at practice in the nets.

LOSS OF FORM

This will happen when a batsman has lost his confidence and is unsure about his ability to play his usual game. He becomes too cautious and over-anxious, and this invariably makes the situation worse. He has problems in scoring runs and then tries to "hit" himself into form, often to no avail.

To overcome the problem, the batsman should aim to play a long innings so that he can become used to the pitch, analyse the bowlers and work out his strategy. He should look to work the ball for quick singles, carefully waiting for the right ball. The longer that the batsman is at the wicket, the easier it becomes to bat. The great South African batsman Graham Pollock has said that a batsman should hardly know that he has hit the ball for the first 20 runs — after that he should start to take control.

It is important first to play the easy shots or the shots you know best. Avoid playing difficult strokes until your confidence returns. Wait. Let the ball come to you. Do not take risks. Relax and let the bat do the work by deflecting and pushing the ball into vacant gaps.

POOR TIMING

Some batsmen will be repeatedly beaten by the bowler because they are not in the correct position to play at the ball. If you are continually missing the ball you will have to improve your concentration. Discipline yourself to pick up the line of the ball more quickly and move behind the line of the ball in time to play the shot intended. If the ball is wide, let it go.

Watch closely every ball that is bowled. Do *not* play premeditated shots before the ball is bowled. Play shots according to what is being bowled.

POOR CONTROL OF STROKES

Sometimes the ball will fly off the edge of the bat or go in a strange direction. This is caused by poor technique, poor timing or bad judgement. The grip could be the problem, or the positioning of the feet and body, or a lapse in concentration. These faults will have to be worked on during practice.

SCORING RESTRICTION

The batsman is prevented from scoring by a well-set and tight field and by accurate bowling. If you are an in-form player you may have to take the initiative and play shots, perhaps hitting over the top of the field — but playing safely and hitting only selected balls.

If facing a spin bowler, "dance" down the pitch to hit the ball on the full or half volley, connecting with it firmly. Sweep good-length balls, provided the line is right. Do not sweep on middle stump because if you miss you could be out lbw.

Facing a fast/medium-pace bowler, use the bat either on an angle or open faced and work or deflect the ball through gully or down fine leg for an easy single. Always look for the quick short single because it can often upset the bowler's line and length and frustrate the fielder. Field changes may have to be made, this could suit the batsman if it gives further gaps in the field through which to hit the ball.

Analysing a bowler

A batsman can pick just what the bowler is trying to do by observing the following:
Ø The grip that the bowler has on the ball: the batsman may be able to see from the grip which way it will swing or spin.
Ø The bowler's run-in. Does he come in

straight most of the time or does he bowl the odd ball from wider out? If an out-swing bowler bowls close to the wicket, the ball will swing more, but if you notice the bowler coming in from a wider angle, the ball will angle in towards you and you will have to play at the ball instead of letting it go.

Ø Changes in the bowling action. If a fast bowler bowls a quicker ball than usual with a wind-up action, pick up the bat earlier than normal. A round-arm delivery will make the ball skid through lower, so be ready to play off the front foot.

Ø The setting of the field. Four slips and a gully means that the bowler will bowl at the off stump to entice you to play the ball into that area. If the ball is wide of the off stump, let it go. If the ball is close to you, keep the face of the bat open and not closed or the ball will be edged into that area.

Ø Changes of pace — the faster or slower ball. The arm action may be slower at the delivery point. Or the bowler may hold the ball further back in the hand than usual to bowl a slower ball.

Points to remember when batting

Ø Concentrate on every ball that is bowled and play the correct shot to the ball that has been bowled. Don't predict or antici-pate what the bowler is trying to bowl. Play each ball on its merits.

Ø Occupy the crease as long as you can and build an innings. The longer that you are at the crease, the easier batting becomes.

Ø Play the innings that the team and the captain requires.

Ø Analyse the pitch conditions and see what the bowler is trying to do before attempt-ing to play many shots.

Ø Watch the ball in the bowler's hand from the time he starts his run-up until the ball hits the middle of the bat.

Ø Analyse the field placements so that you can see where possible runs can be scor-ed. Look to see where the best fielders are positioned and don't take chances with them.

Ø When playing an attacking stroke there is one definite step forward or back — and not both. Don't get caught halfway.

Ø The top hand always controls the bat — don't let the bottom hand push forward in front of the bat to cause an air shot when contact is made.

Ø Keep the head still and the eyes level at all times. Don't lift your head.

Ø Pick up the line of the ball and position the body inside it, with the exception of cross-bat shots such as the sweep, cut, pull or hook.

Ø Where possible keep the ball on the ground and hit in the air only when you have the confidence and ability to hit over the top of the field to the boundary. Don't take the fielder on if he is positioned on the boundary because he will invariably catch you out.

CHAPTER FOUR

BOWLING

More than any other player, the bowler dictates play. His bowling will decide whether runs are scored, wickets fall or defensive shots are played. And because the bowler exerts himself over a sustained period of time, it is the most physically exhausting position as well.

To bowl effectively, a bowler must practise regularly and have control of line and length. If you are starting bowling as a youngster, it is important that you decide what type of bowler you want to be and start developing that style as soon as possible. Later on you may well change your bowling style, but it is best to stick to one kind of delivery at a time rather than a host of variations.

Young bowlers should not try to bowl with a full-sized ball — young fingers are too small and not strong enough to take the strain. For boys 11 years and younger, a 134-gram (4¾ ounce) ball is large enough (and is equally suitable for girls 18 years and younger). For boys 12 years and over, a 156-gram (5½ ounce) normal size ball may be used. Girls 19 and over should use a 142-gram (5-ounce) ball.

The greatest joy in bowling is to see the batsman's wicket being broken. Here I have bowled Greg Chappell for 72 during the third test at Melbourne in 1981.

oping your main skill. For example, say you have a problem with length and are bowling too short. Hold the ball further forward in the fingers and more loosely, and try to bowl six yorkers. Once you have accomplished that try to bowl six good-length balls, then slot in another yorker. Such a programme utilises practice to its best effect and is *developing* your skill.

The grip

Grip will vary depending on the type of ball you bowl.

SWING BOWLING — FAST OR MEDIUM PACE

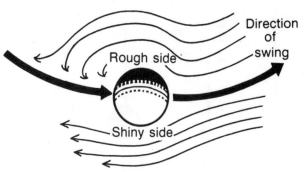

The theory of swing. The ball will swing more consistently if one side of the ball is more shiny than the other. The air on the shiny side flows past the ball relatively undisturbed. However, the air flow on the rougher side and on the seam becomes turbulent. This creates different pressures, causing the ball to swing. The slower the ball is bowled the more chance it will swing because it will be more susceptible to the change in pressure.

OUTSWINGER

Probably one of the most lethal. The ball must be pitched up, tempting the batsman to drive. If the batsman has not got to the pitch of the ball then the outside edge of the bat is often found by the swinging ball and a catch is offered to the slips.

Here I have bowled Jimmy Higgs first ball in the same match.

Again, the length of the pitch will vary with age. The younger you are, the less strength you will have. Bowlers 11 years and under should practice bowling on pitches of 16.44 metres (18 yards); 12–13 year olds on 18.3-metre (20-yard) pitches and 14 years and over on a full-sized 20.13-metre (22-yard) pitch.

Whatever your age, bowl with purpose and spirit. You cannot just hope that things will happen with your bowling — you must *make* them happen! I am a firm believer in the theory that what you put in, you get out. If you bowl with purpose and put a lot of effort into practice you will be rewarded.

In the nets, practise the type of delivery you would bowl in a match. Too many fast bowlers try to bowl spin, to little or no effect. To my way of thinking practice is for devel-

Outswing.

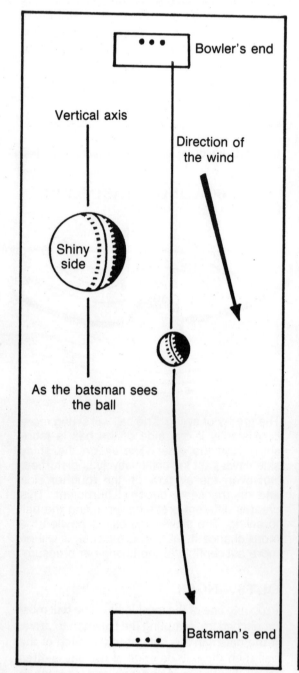

Inswing.

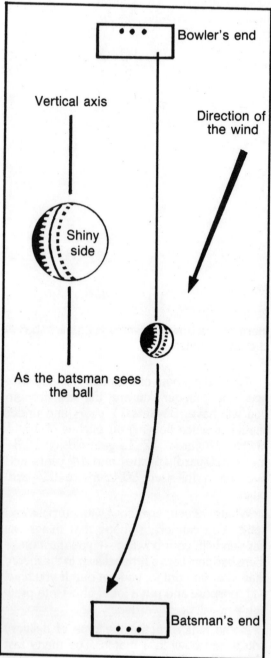

Hold the ball loosely with the tips of the first two fingers close together on either side of the seam and the thumb under the seam of the ball. The body is positioned as side on as possible at delivery. The seam is angled towards first slip. The shiny side of the ball is held to the right-hand side from the bowler's point of view.

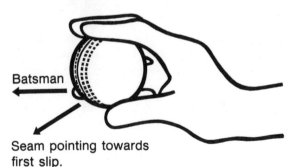

Shiny side of ball

The outswinger. The seam points towards first slip. An alternative grip is to hold the ball directly down the seam with the fingers as close as possible. Make sure the shiny side is on the outside.

Batsman

Seam pointing towards first slip.

The outswinger from another angle.

Bowl from as close to the stumps as possible. At delivery the wrist should lock and the ball will fly away with the seam pointing down the pitch or towards first slip. It is not spun in any way but the fingers cut down very slightly on the outside of the ball. At follow-through the bowling arm cuts across the body and finishes down the left side of the body.

INSWINGER

As its name implies, this ball moves into the batsman's body. Again, the ball is held loosely with the tips of the first two fingers. The first finger is alongside the seam and the second finger on the outside of the seam. The actual seam points towards fine leg. The shiny side of the ball is held to the left-hand side from the bowler's point of view.

At delivery, bowl a little wider of the wickets than the outswingers. The left foot is placed wider than the outswinger and the body arm follows through past the right side of the body and not across to the left side as in the outswinger.

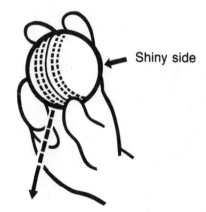

Shiny side

The inswinger. The seam points towards fine leg.

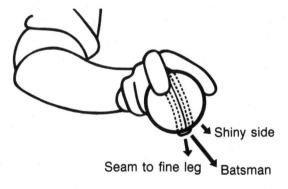

Shiny side

Seam to fine leg   Batsman

The inswinger from another angle. Some bowlers will hold the ball directly down the seam, with their fingers placed close together.

OFF-SPINNER

This ball will spin from left to right, or off to leg. The ball is held on the seam by the index and second finger and with the third finger firmly on the ball. The first or index finger provides the main spin. The seam points towards fine leg as the ball goes down the pitch. The back of the hand faces mid-wicket at delivery. The wrist, at first "cocked" back, then flicks forward with the first finger dragging sharply downwards and the thumb flicking upwards.

The off-spinner. As an alternative grip some bowlers will grip the ball across the seam instead of down it. Using both grips may provide variation.

After delivery, the hand cuts across the body and finishes with the palm pointing upwards. The ball should be pitched on the off to middle stump. (As an alternative, some bowlers will grip the ball across the seam instead of as above. Use both grips for variation.)

OFF-CUTTER

Same grip as for off-spinner but is given a fast off-break delivery. It is frequently used by

The off-cutter. The seam points to fine leg.

medium-pace bowlers. The seam should point to fine leg.

LEG-CUTTER

A medium-pace bowler able to bowl a leg-cutter poses many problems for the batsmen. In effect this ball is a fast leg break, the grip being much the same as for the leg break. However, the cutter is bowled very much from the fingers rather than with the wrist work of the leg break.

The leg-cutter. The fingers roll across the ball to the off side as it is delivered.

If there is bounce in the pitch, the batsman has a great deal of difficulty in playing the ball as it deviates from right to left. The batsman will often offer a catch into the slips area.

The ball is sometimes held across the seam and held quite firmly. The second finger does most of the work, cutting across the ball from right to left, or leg to off. (An alternative grip is to hold the ball down the seam like a swing bowler and allow the fingers to do the work.)

LEG BREAK

This ball turns from right to left and is the hardest ball to bowl because of the high degree of control necessary for accurate flight and direction. If too much emphasis is placed on spin, the ball can easily be dragged down the pitch, allowing the batsman to punish it anywhere around the field. On a turning pitch, however, and with the correct line, length and flight, the batsman can have great difficulty in playing a ball that is leaving him.

The grip used allows for the top joint of the thumb and the first two fingers to spread naturally across the seam. The third finger cups the ball and lies along the seam to impart the spin. The wrist is bent inwards and comes up straight on delivery. The third and fourth fingers flick upwards and forwards whilst the thumb-side of the hand cuts downwards.

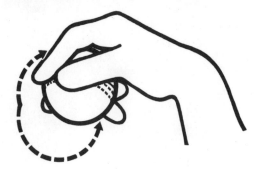

The leg break. The first knuckles of the index finger and the third finger are on the seam. The thumb is merely used to provide balance. The ball is spun, not rolled.

The spin is anti-clockwise and the seam should point towards gully as it goes down the pitch. After delivery the hand finishes with palm downwards. Left-arm leg-spinners grip the ball similarly to an off-spinner.

OVER-SPINNER

This is a top-spinner. The grip is the same as for a leg-spinner except that the seam, instead of pointing to gully, points towards the batsman on the way down the pitch. The ball goes straight and because of the over spin, bounces higher than normal. The back of the hand points to the batsman when delivery is complete.

THE WRONG 'UN OR GOOGLY

The turn is from left to right and the grip is similar to the leg-spinner but with the hand and wrist coming right over so that the back of the hand faces the ground when the ball is released.

The ball is spun off the second and third fingers. The ball is pitched on the off stump or slightly outside so that it will spin back into the batsman. The seam points to fine leg on

the way down. It is a very difficult ball to bowl and the right line and length are vital.

The run-up

MEASURING THE RUN-UP

Too long a run-up can be detrimental to your delivery, particularly in the case of younger bowlers. It may cause you to lose your rhythm and arrive at delivery with a ball of only mediocre pace with little or no accuracy. A maximum of 15 metres is ample for any young bowler.

The run-up should be measured so that the fast bowler does not run out of steam and can still put everything into his last few strides before delivery without falling over or losing his balance at delivery. The key word is "balance"; that is what a run-up is all about — getting you in the right position at the right time to bowl.

Start with your toes or heels on the bowling crease and count the required number of paces back. Put a marker down so that you know where to start your run-in from. You should always measure the same run-up at the start of each spell or at the start of each match. If you vary it you may lose rhythm or bowl too early — or even not at all.

Measured precisely, the correct run-up means that there is no need to look where your feet are going to land at the point of delivery. (Remember, the front foot should cut the batting crease. If your foot goes over the line then that is an illegal delivery and a "no ball" will be called.)

The run-up may be slightly angled, but most coaches would emphasise a straight approach for fast bowlers, while spinners would invariably run in from an angle as this may assist the bowler to get more "side" on at delivery.

A spinner's run-up is very short, but the same principle applies. It should be long enough to help your rhythm so that you are in the right position to bowl comfortably.

This sequence shows the basic bowling action, from the relaxed beginning of the run-up to

the important follow-through.

Dennis Lillee of Australia holds the world record for test dismissals. This magnificent shot shows him in the "take off" position at delivery, both feet off the ground and his balancing left arm about to be unfolded.

RUN TO THE CREASE

You have measured your run-up and have the ball in your hands ready to run in and bowl. At this stage your eyes should be firmly focused on where you want to pitch the ball. If you watch your feet on the run-in and especially at delivery, there is little or no chance of the ball going where you want it to.

For medium-pace and fast bowlers the run-in should be smooth and gradually building up in pace so that you are at your quickest four metres from delivery. The arms should be relaxed and moving rhythmically to help your balance. A fast bowler starts in a slightly crouched or stooping position. As he draws closer to the wicket he will stand more erect to increase his momentum. The key word here is "relaxed". If you are too tense or stiff when running in to bowl, there will be no rhythm and you will find it difficult to bowl accurately.

The basic action

As the bowler approaches the crease he turns sideways, moving his hips and shoulders as side-on as possible. His head is steady, looking over his front shoulder, his eyes level and firmly focused on where he wants the ball to pitch. His free arm starts to point to the sky to provide balance. (If that free arm does not go high enough he will lose balance and lean away. It also assists him in aiming.)

The body weight is now transferred from the back foot to the front foot, the front leg well braced to keep the body in an upright position. If the front leg collapses, then so does the trajectory of the ball. The front arm is now at its highest point — straight up.

The front foot should cut the popping crease. The foot should point down the pitch or to a fine leg position. As the bowler bowls, he will bowl across his front leg.

As the ball is released, the bowling arm cuts across the body and finishes down the opposite side of the body. The bowling arm will come down together with the front arm (balance arm). Remember to keep the front arm up as long as possible so that the body is held in an upright position.

THE FOLLOW-THROUGH

The follow-through is vital to the rhythm of your bowling and cannot be ignored. A fast bowler, for instance, who has just run in at pace for some 15–20 metres, turned sideways and delivered the ball at perhaps 110–140 kilometres per hour, would injure his back if he just stopped "dead". The body must be allowed to unwind.

Generally speaking, a fast bowler should follow-through 6–10 metres, a medium pacer 4–5 metres, and a right-arm leg-spinner 1–2 metres. Some off-spinners may not follow through at all: there is very little pressure placed on their backs.

Always run off the pitch as soon as possible

Dennis Lillee's superb delivery stride. The front leg is high and fully extended, the front arm is reaching for the sky and he is looking over his front shoulder.

Lillee's follow-through is classical. The fully extended left arm helps him to stay upright after delivery. The front foot is still pointing down the pitch and the eyes are still fixed firmly on their target.

when the ball has left your hand. If you run down the pitch and mark it you will damage the pitch for your own batsmen as well as the opposition. The umpires will certainly intervene and tell you to run wider. If you don't, you will get two further warnings; on the third official infringement you can be removed from the bowling crease. The "danger area" is 30.48 centimetres either side of the middle stump and 1.22 metres in front of the popping crease. Keep well clear.

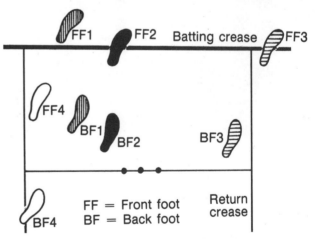

The no ball rule. Positions one and four are no balls. In position one the front foot has landed in front of the batting crease. In position four the back foot has cut or landed on the return crease. (A no ball can also be called if the bowler "throws" the ball at delivery or if there are more than two men fielding behind square on the leg side.)

61

New Zealand opener Bruce Edgar has a batsman's view of Dennis Lillee.

As I climb into my delivery stride in this shot I am about to jump into the air and am already starting to turn into a side-on position.

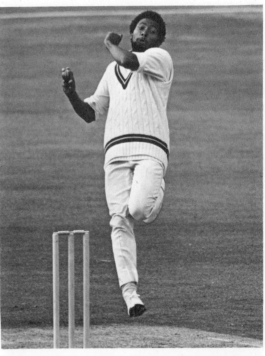

Andy Roberts of the West Indies shows his take-off stride. Note his grip.

The fast bowler must "take off" prior to delivering the ball. In my jump I become more side-on to the batsman.

The fast bowler's action

The greatest demands on action and technique are made by the fast bowler. A pace bowler must put together an explosive sequence of highly co-ordinated movements. His action must develop maximum hand speed, it must be mechanically efficient in order to conserve energy and resist injury, and it must be consistent to ensure accuracy and constant pace.

For a fast bowler to gain maximum speed he must use a minimum of 14 running paces — although 20 paces may be needed by some bowlers.

A recent analysis of the bowling action produced the following information. The force applied to the ball by different parts of the action was broken down into the following percentages:

Ø   Run-in — 19 per cent
Ø   Leg action and hip rotation — 23 per cent
Ø   Trunk flex and rotation of the shoulders — 11 per cent
Ø   Flexing of the shoulder joint — 41 per cent
Ø   Flexing of the wrist — 5 per cent

It has been proven that basic strength is not necessarily a significant factor in the speed of the ball; it is increased co-ordination of the various muscles which increase the ball's pace. Strength will certainly help in the constant repetition of the bowling action before tiredness sets in. Poor timing will also increase fatigue because extra energy will be required to execute an effective delivery (and poor timing is also likely to cause injury).

Flexibility is vitally important in the bowling action. If the muscles have not been stretched or warmed up prior to bowling, they will not function at their maximum efficiency. So it is important to warm up properly. It has been found that if the body temperature is raised by 2°C by a warm-up, the speed of muscle contraction will be increased by nearly 20 percent.

The fast bowler's follow-through. The bowling arm finishes down past the left-hand side of the body while the balancing left arm "reaches for the sky" behind the bowler.

Bowling to a length

There are eight different lengths that a bowler can bowl, but depending on the type of bowler you are you will probably want to bowl only some of them.

Ø *The long hop* is a ball that pitches halfway down the pitch. The batsman will consider it a gift and easy to score from because the ball can be hit almost anywhere. He'll probably pull it on the leg side. The long hop should not, therefore, be bowled.

Ø *Short of a length* — This ball pitches nearer the batsman than the long hop. Although it is short of a correct length it can be used effectively to contain the batsman, and on a difficult pitch it can be a wicket taker.

Ø *Good-length* — The ball is directed either on or just outside the off stump. This is the length that bowlers should be looking to bowl.

Ø *The half-volley* — This ball pitches beyond a good length. Every batsman is looking for this one because it invites an easy scoring shot off the front foot. The batsman looks to hit the ball as it pitches, But the half-volley can also be a wicket-taking ball when a new batsman is at the crease, especially when the ball is swinging. The batsman may not quite get his foot to the ball and may edge it into the slips or mis-time it and loft it into the outfield.

Ø *The yorker* — The ball pitches right at the batsman's feet. It is a very good wicket-taking ball and can easily take the batsman by surprise. He may play directly over the top of it, allowing the ball through onto his stumps or being caught in front lbw. The yorker should be bowled with extra pace. It is a very good ball to bowl when the batsman is looking to score quick runs, because no one can score many, if any runs from a yorker. However, it is a difficult ball to bowl because the margin of error between a yorker and full toss is not great.

Ø *The full toss* — Like a long hop, this is a ball that batsmen call a "gift". The ball does not pitch and the batsman can easily hit it to almost anywhere in the field, depending on the height of delivery.

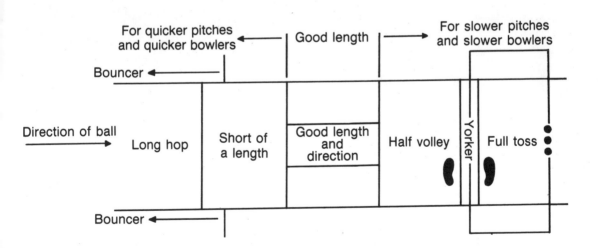

Relative pitching areas for different length deliveries.

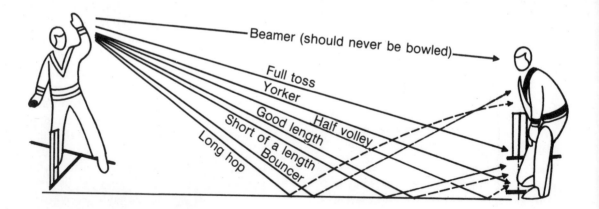

Beamer (should never be bowled)

Full toss

Yorker

Half volley

Good length

Short of a length

Bouncer

Long hop

The different bowling lengths, another view.

The bouncer is a legitimate delivery in the fast bowler's armoury. Derek Underwood has got himself into a real tangle playing this one from Michael Holding of the West Indies.

The bouncer can unsettle a batsman and bring about his dismissal. This one bowled by Australia's Jeff Thomson to John Morrison of New Zealand is a beauty, forcing the batsman to take his eyes off the ball and play a very bad shot.

Ø *The bouncer* — This ball pitches about where the long hop does, but it is bowled at extreme pace and lifts awkwardly onto the batsman's chest or head, forcing him to play a rash shot and generally making life unpleasant. It should be used sparingly because it is more effective when there is an element of surprise.

Ø *The beamer* — This is a head-high full toss and should never be bowled under

any circumstances. It can be a very dangerous delivery, in fact a "killer". The batsman may fail to pick up the line and pace of the ball because it travels that much quicker to the batsman through a direct line. The ball which first bounces allows more time for the batsman to position himself to play his intended shot.

The right length to bowl depends on pitch conditions, the height and reach of the batsman, and the ball. A good-length ball is one that makes the batsman hesitate whether to play back or forward, with the possible result that he remains out of position long enough to make a mistake. By bowling a good length ball the bowler has the best chance of obtaining a wicket.

If the wrong length or line is bowled, then the batsman has the advantage.

Ø A *new* ball should be kept well up to the batsman so that he is brought forward. If the ball swings, the outside edge of the bat could be found or an lbw or bowled could eventuate.

Ø An *old* ball should be pitched slightly short of a length. There will be little or no movement in the air and the ball is not likely to seam off the pitch as much as a new ball.

Ø On a *fast and bouncy pitch* the ball should be kept up to the batsman with the idea of bringing him forward.

Ø On a *slow pitch* the ball should be pitched short of a length. This serves to contain the batsman. His frustration at being tied down and not allowed to score runs may lead to a risky shot and dismissal.

Ø On a *turning pitch* the ball should be kept up to the batsman to bring him forward. (Exact length will be determined by subtle changes in flight and style and by the batsman's technique.)

New Zealand right-arm off-spinner John Bracewell demonstrates his bowling action.

Australia's Bruce Yardley bowls his off-spinners against New Zealand at the Basin Reserve, Wellington. Here he is coming round the wicket, bowling across his front leg. Yardley's front leg should perhaps be more braced, and he does not come from as high as he should.

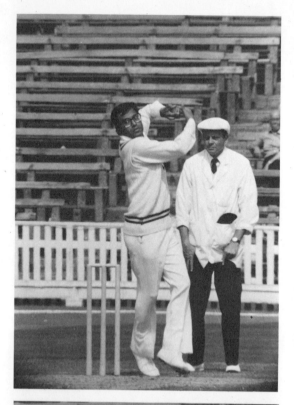

Dilip Doshi has continued the great tradition of Indian spinners, bowling with fine precision with a very simple action. Here he bowls left-arm round the wicket. Notice his side-on position at delivery and his strong follow-through.

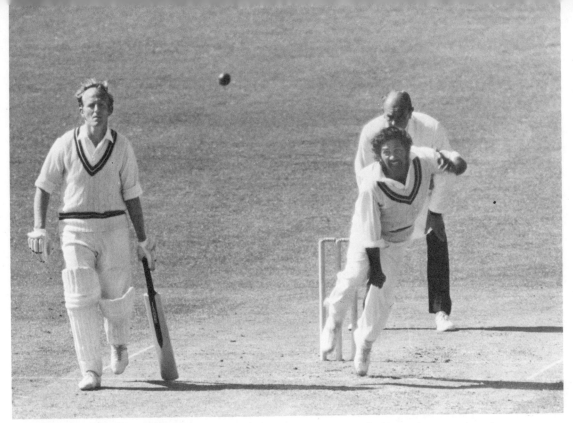

Leg-spinner Mustaq Mohammed of Pakistan follows through strongly.

Intikhab Alam of Pakistan demonstrates the leg-spinner's technique as he bowls over the wicket. Note his grip and the placing of the seam.

USE OF THE BREEZE

If possible, use any breeze that's about to assist your delivery. If you are an outswing bowler you will want the breeze at your back or coming from your right shoulder. Those out-swingers who don't rely on sheer pace and want the ball to hold up a little in the air will prefer the breeze in their face from fine leg or mid-wicket. An inswinger will prefer the breeze from over his left shoulder or from cover or third man.

Spin bowlers will want to use the breeze to drift the ball into or away from the batsman, the ball holding up in the air then dropping quickly through the use of over-spin. If a leg-spinner bowls into the breeze, he will drift the ball *towards* the right-hand batsman. An off-spinner into the breeze will drift the ball *away* from the batsman. Some off-spinners like the wind coming over their right shoulder. Initially the ball will swing further away from the bats-man if the bowler is trying to turn the ball as well. The batsman will find it difficult to play if it spins back into him off the wicket. (The situation is similar for a left-arm leg-spinner with the breeze coming over his left shoulder.)

VARIATION OF PACE AND USE OF THE CREASE

This is the occasional use of a delivery different to that normally bowled. The key to results here is subtlety. The variation should not be over-used, and it should be exploited in such a way that the batsman is surprised.

Change of pace for a fast bowler usually bowling a good length ball on the off stump will include the slower ball, the faster ball, the bouncer and the yorker.

The spin bowler's stock delivery is a good-length ball that pitches on middle and leg or on off. His subtle variation may be the faster, flatter delivery, or a slower one. Very rarely, if at all, would he attempt a bouncer, simply because the wicketkeeper would be standing up behind the wicket and it would be dangerous.

All bowlers should use the crease: i.e., they should bowl close and then wide of the wickets. This alters the angle of delivery and may get a batsman out if he hasn't quite positioned himself or allowed for that slight change. Again, you can run in close to the wickets and at delivery pull out and bowl wide of the wicket. Or vice versa.

FIELD PLACEMENT

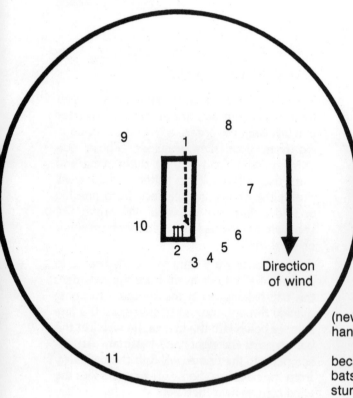

1. Bowler
2. Wicket-keeper
3. First slip
4. Second slip
5. Third slip
6. Gully
7. Cover
8. Mid-off
9. Mid-on
10. Bat/pad
11. Fine leg

Field placement 1: Fast outswing bowler (new ball) bowling with the wind to a right-hand batsman.

The field emphasis will be on the off side because the ball will swing away from the batsman. The bowler should bowl at off stump.

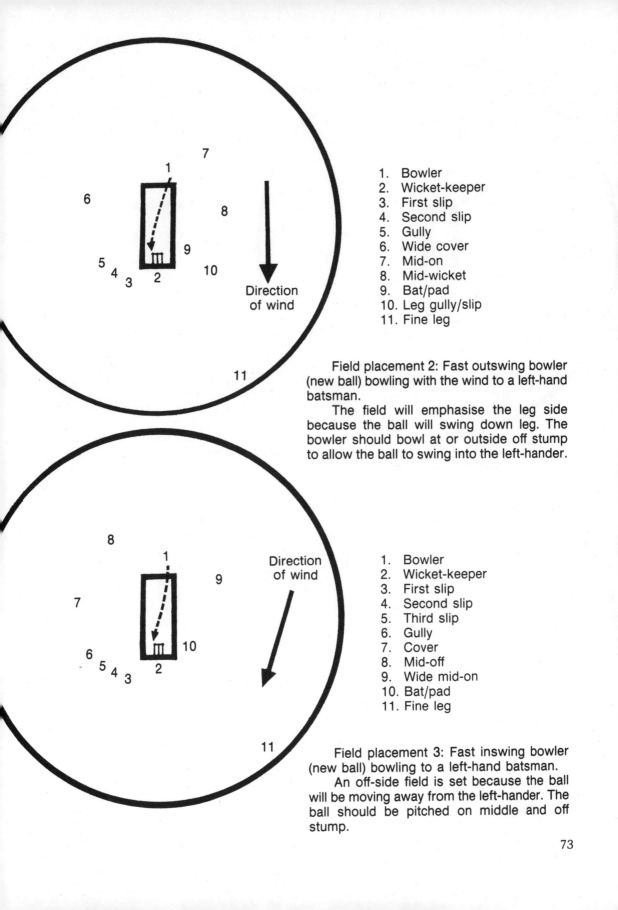

1. Bowler
2. Wicket-keeper
3. First slip
4. Second slip
5. Gully
6. Wide cover
7. Mid-on
8. Mid-wicket
9. Bat/pad
10. Leg gully/slip
11. Fine leg

Field placement 2: Fast outswing bowler (new ball) bowling with the wind to a left-hand batsman.

The field will emphasise the leg side because the ball will swing down leg. The bowler should bowl at or outside off stump to allow the ball to swing into the left-hander.

1. Bowler
2. Wicket-keeper
3. First slip
4. Second slip
5. Third slip
6. Gully
7. Cover
8. Mid-off
9. Wide mid-on
10. Bat/pad
11. Fine leg

Field placement 3: Fast inswing bowler (new ball) bowling to a left-hand batsman.

An off-side field is set because the ball will be moving away from the left-hander. The ball should be pitched on middle and off stump.

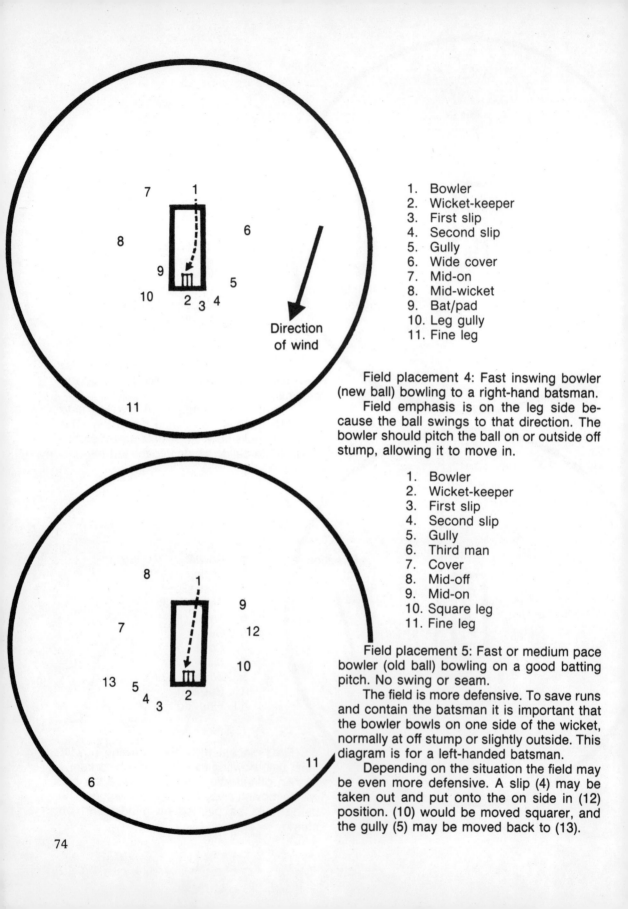

1. Bowler
2. Wicket-keeper
3. First slip
4. Second slip
5. Gully
6. Wide cover
7. Mid-on
8. Mid-wicket
9. Bat/pad
10. Leg gully
11. Fine leg

Field placement 4: Fast inswing bowler (new ball) bowling to a right-hand batsman.

Field emphasis is on the leg side because the ball swings to that direction. The bowler should pitch the ball on or outside off stump, allowing it to move in.

1. Bowler
2. Wicket-keeper
3. First slip
4. Second slip
5. Gully
6. Third man
7. Cover
8. Mid-off
9. Mid-on
10. Square leg
11. Fine leg

Field placement 5: Fast or medium pace bowler (old ball) bowling on a good batting pitch. No swing or seam.

The field is more defensive. To save runs and contain the batsman it is important that the bowler bowls on one side of the wicket, normally at off stump or slightly outside. This diagram is for a left-handed batsman.

Depending on the situation the field may be even more defensive. A slip (4) may be taken out and put onto the on side in (12) position. (10) would be moved squarer, and the gully (5) may be moved back to (13).

1. Bowler
2. Wicket-keeper
3. Slip
4. Gully
5. Point
6. Cover
7. Mid-off
8. Mid-on
9. Mid-wicket
10. Bat/pad
11. Deep backward square leg

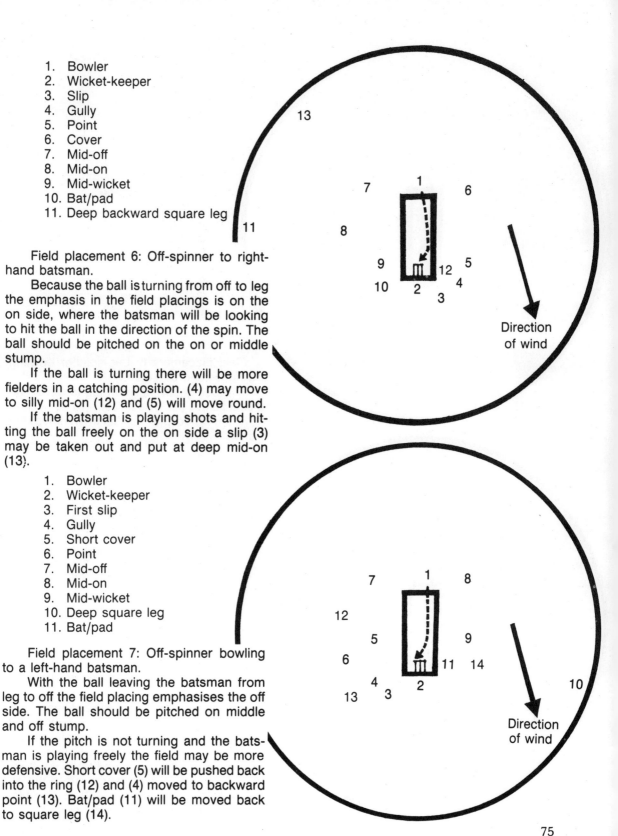

Field placement 6: Off-spinner to right-hand batsman.

Because the ball is turning from off to leg the emphasis in the field placings is on the on side, where the batsman will be looking to hit the ball in the direction of the spin. The ball should be pitched on the on or middle stump.

If the ball is turning there will be more fielders in a catching position. (4) may move to silly mid-on (12) and (5) will move round.

If the batsman is playing shots and hitting the ball freely on the on side a slip (3) may be taken out and put at deep mid-on (13).

1. Bowler
2. Wicket-keeper
3. First slip
4. Gully
5. Short cover
6. Point
7. Mid-off
8. Mid-on
9. Mid-wicket
10. Deep square leg
11. Bat/pad

Field placement 7: Off-spinner bowling to a left-hand batsman.

With the ball leaving the batsman from leg to off the field placing emphasises the off side. The ball should be pitched on middle and off stump.

If the pitch is not turning and the batsman is playing freely the field may be more defensive. Short cover (5) will be pushed back into the ring (12) and (4) moved to backward point (13). Bat/pad (11) will be moved back to square leg (14).

Direction of wind

Direction of wind

75

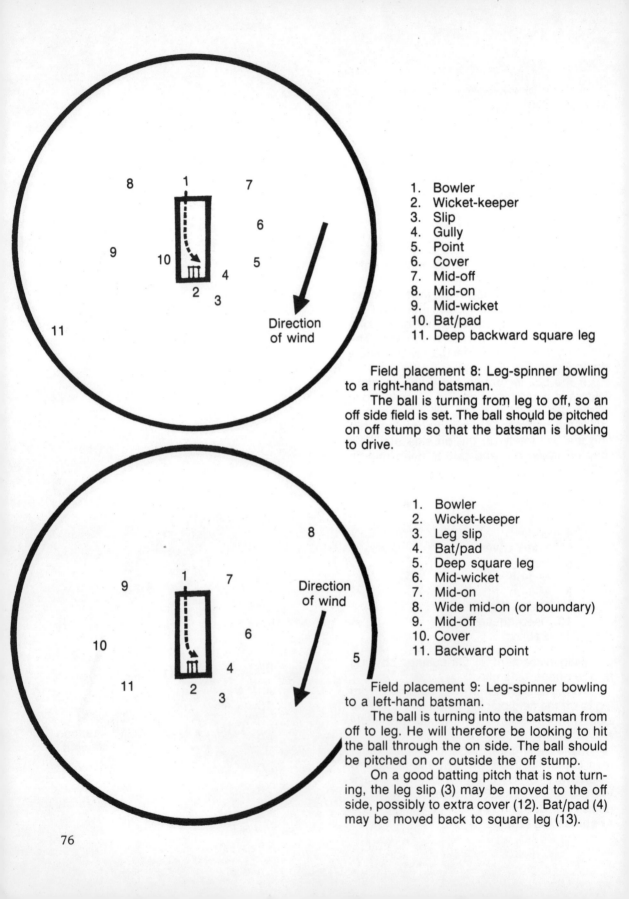

1. Bowler
2. Wicket-keeper
3. Slip
4. Gully
5. Point
6. Cover
7. Mid-off
8. Mid-on
9. Mid-wicket
10. Bat/pad
11. Deep backward square leg

Field placement 8: Leg-spinner bowling to a right-hand batsman.

The ball is turning from leg to off, so an off side field is set. The ball should be pitched on off stump so that the batsman is looking to drive.

1. Bowler
2. Wicket-keeper
3. Leg slip
4. Bat/pad
5. Deep square leg
6. Mid-wicket
7. Mid-on
8. Wide mid-on (or boundary)
9. Mid-off
10. Cover
11. Backward point

Field placement 9: Leg-spinner bowling to a left-hand batsman.

The ball is turning into the batsman from off to leg. He will therefore be looking to hit the ball through the on side. The ball should be pitched on or outside the off stump.

On a good batting pitch that is not turning, the leg slip (3) may be moved to the off side, possibly to extra cover (12). Bat/pad (4) may be moved back to square leg (13).

CHOOSING THE RIGHT END TO BOWL FROM

The use of the breeze is probably the most important aspect to consider initially, but other factors include the slope of the pitch (if any) and whether the pitch is grassier or more bare at one end than the other. If there *is* a slope at one end, you must decide what effect it will have on bowling; e.g., if it is sloping from right to left, it will help the leg-cutter bowler move the ball away from a right-hand batsman towards the slips. It will also assist the leg-spinner the same way. If the pitch is grassy at one end, it will assist the seam bowler. If it is dusty or bare of grass then the spinner will benefit.

MOTIVATION

Every bowler should go out with the desire to get the batsmen out as quickly as possible and to get as many wickets as possible in an innings or match. To be realistic, if a bowler settles for four or five wickets a match, he has done very well. There are some games in which you may only pick up one wicket, while in others you'll have a field day and pick up nine or ten. Take advantage of the good days and when the season is over, look back and see if you have achieved on average your target strike rate.

To help me achieve my target rate I have four key words that constantly remind me of what I have to do as a bowler:

— Lillee

— Hate

— Rhythm

— Off stump

Dennis Lillee is a player I have long admired. He is aggressive, confident and competitive, and has the will and desire to be successful. When the game has not gone well, I often think to myself "What would Lillee do?" One thing is for sure — he would never give up.

Foster an objective hate for the batsman.

He should be someone you want to remove because he is an obstacle to you and the team. Life should not be made easy for him.

Rhythm: bowling is all about rhythm, timing and co-ordination. You do not need to be big and strong to bowl fast. You have to relax when bowling. A bowler who is too tense and stiff can drag the ball down into the pitch and bowl wide.

Off stump is simply the target area for the line I want to bowl. This may vary depending on the batsman's technique.

Perhaps the greatest fast bowler in the history of cricket demonstrates his classical action. "I often think to myself 'What would Lillee do?' "

"Reading" a batsman

A bowler can analyse a batsman's technique before he has even bowled a ball. If he has the ability to "read" that technique he will be able to bowl a correct line and length.

⊘ A tall batsman will have a long reach and will be a front foot player. He will be looking to drive and push forward, to prevent lbw decisions. It is important to bowl short of a length, and to keep him more on the back foot and on the defensive.

⊘ A small batsman. The ball should be pitched further up to bring him forward. Because of his shorter reach he may not quite get to the pitch of the ball.

⊘ A batsman with a crouched stance and low grip on the bat handle is looking to get under the ball to hook or over the ball to cut. He will be a bottom-hand player, meaning that he will hit the ball in the air a lot. The ball should be kept up to him to cramp him so that he doesn't hook or cut. Make sure that he is brought forward to drive.

⊘ A batsman with his hands apart on the bat handle will look to scoop the ball around on the leg side or cut on the off. He will also push at the ball; if his bottom hand dominates (as it will on most occasions) the ball will go in the air if his timing is just a little bit out. This type of player will struggle on a wet or slow pitch because the ball won't come onto the bat. The bowler should pitch his deliveries on a good length or short of a length.

⊘ A batsman with an open stance is looking to hit the ball on the leg side. His bat is lifting in the direction of gully; when it comes down the face is angled towards the on side. It is important to bowl outside off stump to eliminate this batsman's strength. His body positioning and head will be out of alignment with the ball; he tends to play away from his body and could easily nick the ball into slips.

⊘ A batsman with a crouched stance and low grip on the bat handle is looking to get under the ball to hook or over the ball to cut. He will be a bottom-hand player, meaning that he will hit the ball in the air a lot. The ball should be kept up to him to cramp him so that he doesn't hook or cut. Make sure that he is brought forward to drive.

⊘ A batsman with a high stance and high grip on the bat is always looking to drive the ball. It is therefore important to bowl short of a length to prevent him pushing forward.

⊘ A batsman with angled bat in the stance (i.e., the face of the bat is too open and is facing the gully position) is a player who deflects the ball through that area. It would pay to add an extra slip or gully because the ball could go in the air through that area, especially with the new ball. Always attack his off stump because while it may be a strength it could easily be a weakness.

⊘ A batsman batting outside the crease is trying to eliminate an lbw decision and get to the pitch of the ball easier. He will be a front player, so bowl short of a length. If possible get the keeper to stand up to the stumps, hopefully forcing the batsman to bat inside his crease.

⊘ A batsman taking a middle stump guard wants the bowler to bowl straight at him so that he can hit the ball straight to mid-on/mid-off, etc. He will also look to work the ball on the leg side if the line is a little wayward. He will be a good judge of letting the ball go outside the off stump, so it is important to bowl directly at off stump, to commit him to playing a shot. Bowl on a good length or just short of length.

⊘ A batsman taking a leg stump guard is more of an off-side player. Anything going down the leg side will be whipped away for easy runs. Bowl at off stump and don't give him room to play freely outside the off stump. Early on in his innings it may pay to bowl a little wider, because he may chase the ball and not get to the pitch of it, thus edging it into the slips. As his innings progresses, a tighter line and length is needed. From a bowler's point of view it should be a great sight to see all three wickets because the batsman has exposed the target that you are trying to hit.

TYPES OF BATSMEN

As the batsman's innings progresses the type of player he is becomes more evident. You should bowl accordingly.

∅ A low backlift means that he is a pusher and deflector. Bowl very close to his body, crowding him and bowl just short of a length. Anything very short will be guided away off the back foot.

∅ A high backlift means that he is a striker of the ball looking to hit through and over the top of the field. Again the bowler should bowl short of a length. More importantly, changes of pace are necessary, especially if he is driving a lot.

∅ If the batsman is driving well and scoring runs freely, then the ball is being over pitched and should be bowled shorter. Change of pace is needed here.

∅ If the batsman is hooking and cutting a lot, the ball has been pitched too short and should be bowled further up.

∅ If the batsman does not play forward or backward and walks across in front of his wickets, it is very important to bowl well up to him. We call him a "shuffler"; bowlers should like bowling to these batsmen because they expose themselves to a bowled and lbw decision. Bowl straight at middle stump.

∅ A batsman who backs away from the ball towards square leg is a bowler's dream. He is obviously frightened of the ball, so the bowler has a great chance of getting him out easily. It is important to bowl at leg stump to cramp the player. In backing away he is giving himself room to swing at the ball, often hitting it in the air. If you

bowl wide of the off stump he has a free arc to swing the ball in any direction. Lbw and bowled decisions are a common dismissal here. These batsmen also tend to get caught at long on, mid-on and cover.

∅ Some batsmen commit themselves to playing a shot before a ball has been bowled by pushing their front foot forward. In this case, the bowler must bowl short of a length to prevent him from driving, and bowl wide of the off stump. The batsman then has to make a secondary movement to get into the correct position. If he is not in the right position he could be caught behind.

Some random notes

1. Bowling to an in-form batsman can be very soul destroying for a bowler, but you just have to keep at it. Instead of trying to get him out, you have to be prepared to sit back and wait until he makes a mistake and gets himself out. Bowl very defensively to a well-set field and try to restrict his scoring shots. Your captain may be prepared to set a deep field to give him one run so that he loses the strike. Then you can attack more by bringing the field in and preventing the other batsman from getting a run.

2. An out-of-form batsman must be pressurised as soon as he comes to the wicket: tight attacking bowling to an attacking field.

3. Bowling too full means that you are letting the ball go too soon. Let the ball leave your hand a little later at delivery.

4. Bowling too short means that you are dragging the ball down the pitch by letting it leave the hand too late. Gripping the ball too tightly will also cause you to drag the ball downwards. Hold the ball further forward in your hand and more loosely.

5. Many right-arm outswing bowlers have difficulty bowling to a left-hand batsman be-

Lance Cairns of New Zealand is a very unorthodox bowler. He bowls off the wrong foot, and with a windmill action. His action is all "front on" — note how he looks through his shoulder instead of over it. This unusual action enables him to bowl huge inswingers.

Australian fast bowler Jeff Thomson achieves extra pace with an arched back and a slinging bowling action.

cause they naturally drift the ball leg side. This will be accentuated if the bowler bowls close to the wickets, as he would do if bowling an outswinger to a right-hand batsman. Left-hand batsmen become very good leg side players because the ball is always on their legs. The bowler must take the initiative by bowling very wide of the crease, angling the ball away towards slips across the batsman. The ball will not swing (not as much anyway) and most left-handers are weak outside the off stump. They will chase at wider balls that leave them and if they have not judged the line, length and angle of the ball they will invariably get caught in the slips/gully area.

6. If as a swing bowler you are finding you cannot control the ball because of excessive movement, grip it across the seam. The ball will not swing. Once you have your line and length under control, try to grip the ball in the normal way.

COMMON FAULTS IN BOWLING

Ø Not having a consistent and gradually accelerating run-up that allows for a good take-off from the left foot to give you height at delivery.

Ø Gripping the ball too tightly, which tends to drag the ball down the pitch.

Ø Lack of concentration — not having your eyes firmly fixed on where you want the ball to land for good line and length.

Ø Not landing with the back foot parallel to the bowling crease with the hips and shoulders not turned sideways.

Ø Insufficient "lean-back" at delivery, away from the batsman. Rocking motion allows for greater pace and control.

Ø Bowling off the wrong foot — complete lack of rhythm, timing and co-ordination.

Ø The front arm not high enough, causing the bowler to lose his balance and fall away at delivery.

Ø The head moves instead of remaining still and level. The eyes should be looking straight down the pitch over the front arm. With faster bowlers the head is slightly angled to allow the bowling arm to reach its highest point.

Ø The front foot lands too wide of the wickets and is openly splayed, pointing to gully, instead of pointing down the pitch.

Ø No follow-through, thus losing rhythm.

Ø Falling over in delivery stride and thus losing balance and control.

Important points to remember:

Ø Control line and length.

Ø Keep sideways as long as possible.

Ø Keep your head still. Think and look where you want the ball to pitch.

Ø Vary your pace and the flight of the ball.

Ø Use the crease to change the angle of delivery.

Ø Follow through after each delivery.

Ø Always run off the pitch and not on or down it.

Ø Know your own field placements.

Ø Consult your captain if any field changes are required.

Ø Keep your cool when bowling. Don't become too frustrated and over-react if decisions go against you or if the batsman is taking the initiative.

CHAPTER FIVE

FIELDING

Good fielding develops team spirit and motivation and wins matches. There is nothing more inspiring than seeing team mates dive around the field to cut off a certain boundary, or take a brilliant catch, or retrieve, pick up, turn and throw the ball over the top of the stumps and run out an unsuspecting batsman.

Fielding involves immense concentration, anticipation, agility and motivation to stay completely alert and active. It is a side of the game often neglected by players wanting to develop their batting or bowling skills. There is no doubt in my mind that if it comes to choosing one player over another of equal batting and bowling ability the player with the better standard of fielding will get the nod. Each team practice session should involve at least a 30-minute fielding session.

Derek Randall of England is probably the finest fielder in the world today. He "smells" out the ball, pounces on it and swiftly returns it to the top of the wickets, often breaking the wicket, in fact, to run out the batsman. He is absolutely deadly from 20 metres and batsmen are wary of his lithe, athletic and agile figure. He chases the ball hard and has the ability to throw on the turn, a quality not many fielders have.

Techniques vary with the different fielding positions. To be a slips, gully or close-in catching fielder you have to be a specialist and possess tremendous reflexes, good eyesight and total concentration. A cover fieldsman also has to anticipate and move quickly — many cheeky runs are stolen by pushing the ball out slowly to the cover area. Generally speaking, the boundary at fine leg or third man is frequently patrolled by fast bowlers. There they

get a little rest period yet still have to be alert for deflections. They must move quickly and, more importantly, need a strong arm to throw the ball 70 metres back to the keeper.

High catching, illustrated by Englishman Derek Randall. When the ball is hit high the fieldsman should try to judge the catch so that he is directly under the line of the ball. The catch should be taken at eye level.

Catching in the outfield

The fielder should watch the ball all the way into his hands and let his hands "give" with the ball when catching. Ideally, the player taking the catch is placed so that he is well balanced, with both feet on the ground, directly under the line of the ball and catching at eye level. You may sometimes have to take a running catch. Move swiftly to get into the best possible position you can — and then good luck.

The hands should "give" into the chest as the catch is taken.

Catching close to the wicket

Close-catching ability is possibly more important than taking outfield catches because of the greater number of chances offered to fielders of the former. Frequently the ball is edged into the slips area or popped up in the air off the bat or glove to silly mid-on or silly mid-off.

Slips fielders should not stand too close. An arm's distance is a good guideline and slips should stagger their positions.

The actual positioning from the wickets depends on pitch conditions and the mood of the bowler. On a hard, fast, bouncing pitch, the fast bowler may be getting lethal pace and lift. The slips will stand back perhaps 15 metres. On a low, slow, docile pitch, they will stand up a lot closer so that when the edge is found, the ball will carry comfortably to them at waist height.

The first slip should be watching the ball while the other slips, gully and bat/pad catchers should watch the edge of the bat and stand with their body weight evenly balanced on the balls of their feet — *not* the heels. They should be in a comfortable and relaxed position, legs apart, knees bent, hands poised ready to catch and with hands and elbows clear of the body.

Bat/pad catchers should watch the batsman's footwork and bat and stay down in a crouched position while the shot is being played — most catches will be close to the ground. By watching the batsman's movements, close-in fielders can determine the type of shot likely to be played and can ready themselves for catching opportunities.

Close-in fielders should always wear a "box" or abdominal protector. A helmet is also recommended, and even shin-guards.

Close-in catching – the ready position. Derek Randall's body weight is on the balls of his feet, allowing for quick movement in any direction.

Some close-in catches have to be taken chest high. Here Derek Randall's fingers are facing upwards with the palms facing the ball.

Slip catch. As the ball is caught waist high the body has risen from the crouched position. It is easier to come up to the ball than to go down to it.

Slip fieldsmen need fast reflexes. Here Derek flings out a hand to take the ball and is diving as he catches it.

The Australian slip cordon at the ready: Greg Chappell at first slip, alongside Alan Border, Kim Hughes and Graham Wood. All are crouched to move up or down easily to take the catch.

Ian Chappell takes his 100th test catch as he holds this one from Lawrence Rowe of the West Indies. From the normal crouched position he has risen with the ball and taken it well.

Ian Botham catches Chetan Chauhan of India off the bowling of Bob Willis. He has moved to his right to get into line with the ball.

Australia's Graeme Wood appeals for a bat/pad catch from the bowling of Bruce Yardley against New Zealand. It is important to be fully protected in this close-in position with protective helmet and visor. Some fielders even wear shin pads as extra protection.

Stopping the ball by using the feet in a "V" position. This method can be used when the ball is hit softly and the fieldsman has plenty of time.

The barrier style, used when the ball is hit very firmly and extra body protection is needed to stop it. This is the safest and most effective method.

Using the foot as a second line of defence. This method is generally used when the fieldsman is approaching the ball on the run to return it quickly to the keeper.

Stopping the ball

Outfielders should walk in with the bowler so that they are mobile and not flat-footed as the ball is bowled. They are then ready to move in any direction, to stop, turn and chase the ball. They are alert and anticipate the ball coming their way every time.

Get your body behind the line of a running ball. There are three methods of stopping the ball so that if you miss it with your hands, your body will prevent the ball from running away for extra runs.

Ø Place your feet in a "V" position behind the line of the ball.

Ø Place your right foot and left leg in such a position that it forms a barrier at right angles to the line of the ball.

Ø When running in towards the ball, place at least one foot behind the line of the ball.

Always use your body as a second line of defence.

The ball should be picked up just in front of your toe(s). Keep your eye on the ball all the way. If you take your eye off it you could misfield.

Someone should be in a backing-up position to prevent overthrows or extra runs. Backing up also helps players maintain interest in the game because it allows for team work and for players to be continually alert.

He has the ability to throw perfectly while still mobile.

Derek has expertly gathered the ball and is about to throw while still in a running position.

The low, flat throw to the keeper. In this example Derek has actually thrown off the back foot, which is difficult to do well if speed and accuracy are to be retained.

West Indian captain Clive Lloyd, known as "The Cat", is ready to return the ball while still on the move. In his earlier days he was one of the most exciting fielders the world has seen.

COMMON FAULTS IN FIELDING

Ø Lack of concentration, causing misfields and dropped catches.

Ø Hands don't "give" with the ball when catching.

Ø Body is not behind the line of the ball to act as a second line of defence.

Ø Not backing up to prevent overthrows.

Ø Moving too slowly towards the ball.

Ø Not moving in with the bowler.

Ø Not watching the captain for fielding adjustments.

Ø Slipsmen fielding too close together.

Ø Unnecessarily hard throwing to the keeper.

Ø Taking too long to throw the ball in by running too far before throwing.

Ø Not looking at the target when throwing.

Ø Incorrect grip of the ball when throwing. (Always grip the ball across the seam, not down it, or the ball may swing from its target.)

Ø Not keeping your eyes on the ball until it is safely in your hands.

Underarm throw to the keeper. Derek Randall approaches the ball crouched low. As he picks up the ball his body weight is on the right foot. The ball is released hard and flat at about waist height, the head behind the line of the ball.

CHAPTER SIX

WICKETKEEPING

A specialist and testing position, wicketkeeping is one that requires great alertness. The good keeper can, given half a chance, be responsible for a quick dismissal. The brilliant catch or stumping can do much to generate team enthusiasm and motivation. The good keeper will tidy up the general standard of fielding by taking the ball neatly and correctly and looking efficient behind the stumps.

Wicketkeeping fundamentals

Alertness — the keeper always ready for the main chance or the inaccurate delivery, particularly when a new-ball bowler is bowling. Then there is more chance of a snick or a delivery moving sharply in the air or off the pitch.

Concentration — watching every ball bowled right from the bowler's hand, as well as every ball that is returned to him from the fieldsmen.

Agility and good reflexes.

Liaising with the bowler — talking to the bowler about the batsmen's weaknesses, the right length to bowl, and perhaps subtle variations of pace. There may be an opportunity of a possible leg-side stumping off a seam bowler; a signal should be given so that the keeper is aware of the possibility.

Setting an example for fielding standards — Be neat and tidy. Catch and stop every ball in the right position. Try to anticipate a bad return and move into position to prevent such throws over-running.

A good standard of equipment — your own gloves, if possible, because the familiarity will help confidence. If you are wearing gloves slightly bigger than usual, you may have difficulties in being efficient. Gloves should always be in good condition. The face of the gloves (the rubber part) should never be allowed to become smooth and shiny; this will make it easier to drop the ball, especially the new ball. Inner gloves should be worn at all times to protect and cushion the hands. Pads should be extremely light and not too big. Boots should be light and well sprigged in sole and heel.

Decisiveness — If you are going for the catch then go in fully. A half movement but then letting the ball go could put off first slip and result in a possible dropped catch.

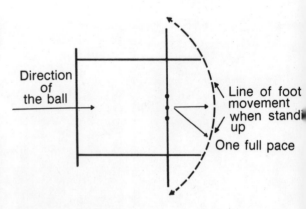

The movement of the keeper (right-hand dotted line) should be up and across in a semi-circle behind the stumps, not backwards. The keeper's feet are one pace behind the stumps.

New Zealand test keeper Ian Smith illustrates the basic keeper's position. The head is still, the eyes level, the body weight on the balls of the toes and the gloves open-faced at ground level.

Ian Smith takes the ball outside the off stump. His eyes are on the ball at all times, watching it into the gloves.

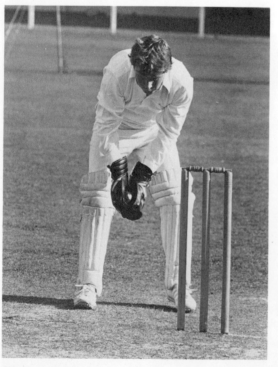

Rod Marsh of Australia is well balanced and perfectly positioned behind the wickets to a spin bowler. The batsman is Lance Cairns of New Zealand.

Marsh has moved down the leg side to take a ball that may have beaten Bruce Edgar. He has picked up the line of the ball and moved quickly into position.

Marsh moves low to his left to take the ball one-handed. He has been positive in going for the ball and Greg Chappell at first slip has moved out of his way.

Ian Smith standing back. As the ball is bowled he rises with it, moving into the line of the ball.

Technique

When catching, let your hands "give" with the ball. Taking the ball properly in this way means there is less chance of damaging your fingers or hands. If the hands are still, rigid or tense the ball is more likely to rebound. Always watch the ball into the gloves.

The fingers should point down, upwards or sideways when taking the ball — *not* at the ball. Fingers pointing at the ball will make it more difficult to catch, and there is increased risk of mistiming and consequent injury. Never snatch at the ball; let it come to you.

The keeper's stance should be a relaxed and comfortable one. He must be already crouched when the bowler runs into bowl. His feet should be about 45 centimetres apart and his body weight on the balls of his feet, not the heels.

When keeping to fast bowlers, stand back from the stumps. As the ball is bowled, rise with it and be directly behind it. Move into position. Sometimes you may have to dive to take a wide delivery or possible snick, but that

should be only in extreme situations. If you are light on your feet then you should be able to move quickly into position to take the ball without having to dive.

Your standing position will depend on pitch conditions and how a bowler is bowling: stand where you can take the ball waist high.

When keeping to spin bowlers, stand up behind the wicket. After staying down for as long as possible, rise with the ball. Your movement should be up and across for the leg or off side delivery, not backwards. Mark a line where your feet should be positioned. When you are keeping to a right-hand batsman and a right-arm bowler your left foot should be on the middle and off stump and your right foot outside the off stump.

Stand 30 centimetres or so behind the stumps, depending on your reach and size. If you stand too far back you could miss a stumping chance or a quick snick. If you stand too close you will knock off the bails with your gloves or pad, or take the ball in front of the stumps.

The head should be positioned straight and still with the eyes level.

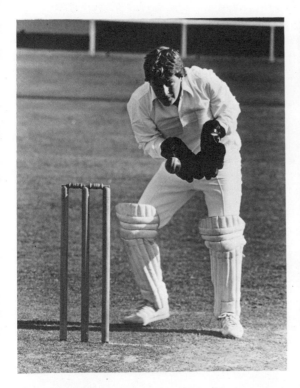

Ian Smith takes the ball down the leg side. He is perfectly balanced as he moves to break the wicket.

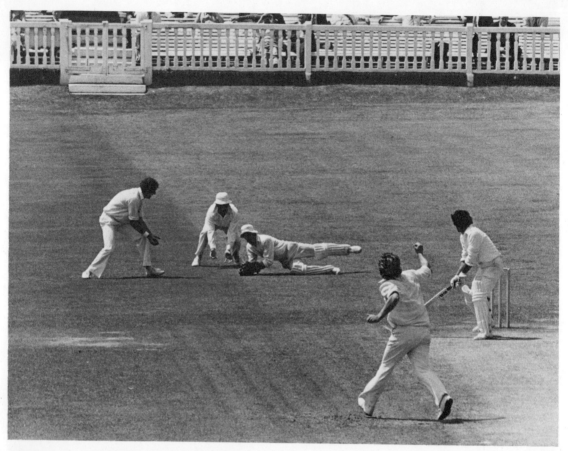

Bob Taylor of England dives to his right to take a low catch from Wasim Bari of Pakistan that probably would not have carried to Mike Brearley at first slip.

COMMON FAULTS WITH WICKETKEEPERS

Ø Standing in "no man's land", neither right up or right back.

Ø Snatching and grabbing at the ball.

Ø Taking eyes off the ball.

Ø Getting up early when standing up to the wicket.

Ø Taking the ball off balance.

Ø Moving to either side too early, before picking up the true line of the ball.

Ø Excessive head movement.

Ø Incorrect weight distribution when attempting to break the wicket.

Ø Casual or even lazy footwork.

Ø Fingers rather than palms pointing at the ball.

Ø Hesitation in going for wide balls.

Ø Unnecessary use of the pads instead of gloves.

Ø Bad returns to the bowler or fielder.

Ø Poorly cared-for equipment.

Ø Loss of concentration.

CHAPTER SEVEN

RUNNING BETWEEN WICKETS

Being run out is the worst dismissal for a batsman. It is a waste of a wicket and games can be lost because of this stupidity. On the other hand it is a great sight watching two batsmen run well between the wickets, stealing cheeky but safe singles, turning twos into threes and annoying the fielding side with their skill.

Calling

There are only three calls in the game of cricket — "yes", "no", or "wait". Youngsters in particular will say "stay", "come on" or some other indecisive call. Provided the striker has a good view of the ball, he should make

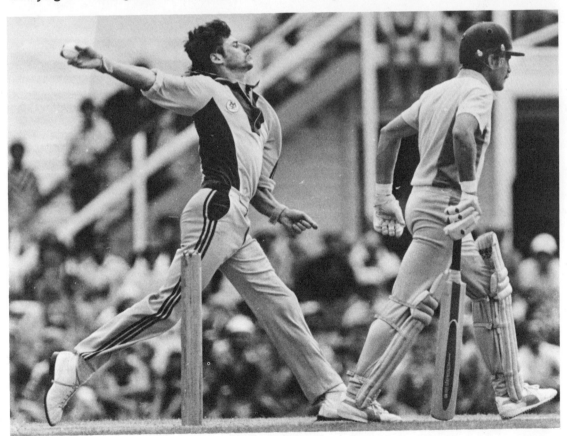

Australian opener Bruce Laird is backing up perfectly, ready to take a quick single. When the ball has left the bowler's hand he should be out of his crease.

a clear and early call: "yes" for a run, "no" if not running, "wait" if he is not sure and then a "yes" or "no" call to follow.

Youngsters should get into the habit of calling after every ball has been bowled. Generally speaking the striker calls when the ball is hit in front of the wicket and the non-striker calls when the ball is hit or passes behind the striker's wicket. Always guarantee your partner a safe passage to the other end. The player running to the danger end generally does the calling for subsequent runs.

Back up

The non-striker should back up at all times. Of course he must take care not to leave his crease until the ball has been bowled or the bowler may run him out.

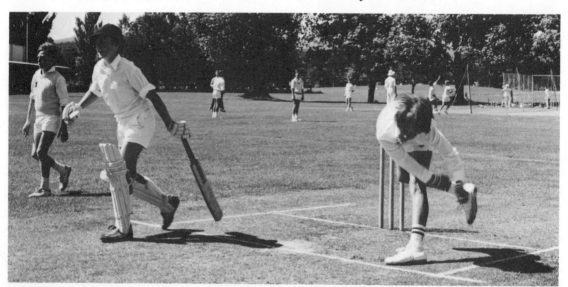

Backing up, the correct way.

The incorrect way. The batsman is in no position to run a quick single.

100

When taking a run under pressure the bat should be slid into the crease along the ground.

The incorrect way. The batsman is out because although he has reached the crease he has not grounded his bat.

Run fast

Always run the first run hard as though it is the winning run. Nearly 25 per cent of all runs are scored through singles. A misfield may give you more time to take a second run.

Slide your bat

Both batsmen should slide their bat over the batting crease. The bat or part of the batsman's body has to be grounded over the line for a run to be scored. Many young cricketers will actually pass over the line with their feet when taking more than one run. This is not necessary. By doing this you are running a greater distance and taking longer over your run. It could result in your being run out.

Note field placings and fielders

Look where the fielders are positioned so that you can best place the ball for possible runs. Note also their various abilities — those with good throws won't allow you to run on the throw, and those who are slow movers in the field may allow an extra run to be taken.

View the ball when turning

Don't turn blind. When turning for a run always view the ball so that you know where it is and how close the fielder is to the ball before he throws it. If necessary change hands with the bat so that it helps your positioning.

CHAPTER EIGHT

CAPTAINCY

The best player is not necessarily the best captain. Often, however, the best player is given the job, and while he is thinking about making various match decisions his own form suffers. The team will miss out both ways if this happens — there will be a lack of good decision making, plus a decline in the captain's personal performance — which will further affect his captaincy.

The captain's role

It is easy to captain the side when things are going well and you have good players in your side. But the test of a real captain comes when things start to go badly. Then he must use his skill and initiative to sort the game out.

The captain should be an easy, outgoing person who can communicate with all his team mates — communication not just in terms of the game but socially as well, as "one of the boys". If he can do this he will usually win the respect of his team, along with their united determination to do well. The captain leads by example, setting standards on such things as arrival time for practices and matches and standard of dress. A sloppy captain will mean a sloppy and undisciplined team. If he is punctual and well attired he can expect everyone to do the same.

At team talks the captain should clearly outline the team strategy for the session or the day's play. After firmly establishing his own plan he should invite comment from his players. He needs their backing and support. If there is disagreement with his plan, it is left to the captain either to review his plan and make changes, or to go ahead with his original

idea. His is the final decision and the team must support it whether they totally agree or not. If that support is not there the team will not function correctly and any chance of success will be diminished.

Criticism of individual or team play should be constructive, not destructive. If something has gone drastically wrong the captain should analyse the situation and come up with a solution. For example, a poor team batting display could have been caused by reckless shots outside the off stump, no one taking it upon their shoulders to show a fighting innings and repair the damage. The captain may well blast his team for that error, but he should then demand more application and dedication to the job in hand. "Occupation of the crease is of vital importance. I do not want to see any batsman flash at a ball outside the off stump until he has scored 50."

Solve a problem with a solution.

Become knowledgeable about the game. This comes through player experience, reading books, listening, observing other captains make decisions and understanding why those decisions have been made.

Learn how to read pitches, set fields, know when to declare, change the batting order if necessary, and know the capabilities of team mates to get the best out of them. Familiarise yourself with the laws of the game and with any special rules pertaining to the game being played, including special conditions at the ground.

Be positive in your approach to the game, always trying for a win if you have a reasonable chance. Play the game hard but within the laws of the game. Remember that the captain who is negative in field placings, who does not make declarations or who uses his pace bowlers too much to slow the game down produces a game that is boring for players and spectators. And spectators expect to be entertained.

Know how to handle team mates. Because they differ in their personalities they will respond differently to the same situation. Two bowlers may be having a difficult time with line and length and the batsmen may be taking control. One of the bowlers may be easily upset and will need to be treated with quiet encouraging words. The other bowler, a more fiery character, may well need a harsh telling off. He will respond to the captain's challenge because he wants to prove that he can do the job — and because he is probably annoyed at being spoken to in that manner. Generally, however, praise and encouragement are the best team and individual motivation tools available.

At the conclusion of the game the captain should offer congratulations or condolences to the opposing captain and thank him for the game. This is a courtesy that should not be neglected. The test and first-class captain may have to be available to the news media for after-match comments on the day's play. If this happens he should be frank and honest in his day's appraisal of the game but careful not to offend or put his own players down. He may well note those individuals who have done especially well, but he shouldn't denigrate those who have failed.

The basic decisions facing captains include the following:

Ø The toss. Assuming you win the toss, do you bat or bowl first?

Ø The batting order.

Ø How do you use your bowlers to best effect?

Ø Correct field placements depending on the type of bowler and situation of the game.

Ø Declarations.

Ø Team and individual discipline.

Ø Team warm-up and proper pre-match training before the game starts.

Ø Recalling the batsman.

The more advanced captain who plays three-day, first-class and five-day test matches may have further to consider:

Ø Final team selection if asked by the selectors.

Ø The correct use of the roller between innings.

Ø Taking the second new ball.

Ø Appealing against the light.

Ø Forfeiting an innings to achieve a result.

Ø Playing in treacherous or wet conditions.

The vice-captain, appointed prior to the match, should be aware of the captain's tactics — he may have to take over if the captain has to leave the field of play for some reason.

The toss

If he wins the toss the captain must decide whether he wants to bat or bowl first. His decision will take into account the pitch conditions, his team's strength, the opposition's strengths and weaknesses, and the state of the competition.

If the pitch is green and fast it should suit his seam bowlers, so he may decide to bowl first to take advantage of the fresh pitch.

If the opposition lacks a good bowling attack he may decide to bat first while the pitch is in its best condition and capable of giving a big score.

If the pitch is bare of grass the captain will bat first. At the end of the fourth innings the pitch will be at its worst and the ball may be turning sharply, making the life of a batsman difficult.

The weather will also be a factor in the decision. On a dull, cloudy or humid day the ball should swing in the air. That could influence the captain to bowl first. If it is a hot, dry day then movement in the air will be less and the captain may decide to bat first. Hot days tend to break the pitch up; after hours of play it may crumble, thus assisting spin bowling. On the other hand, cooler dull days tend to preserve the freshness in the pitch and bind the pitch together, which should suit medium-pace bowlers with seam. Such a pitch is also a good batting pitch, however, and the captain's decision in this case may depend on the other factors.

Generally speaking, the captain will bat first in a one-day game provided conditions are equal for both sides. The pitch conditions and weather will be unchanging throughout the day's play. If a good score is achieved there will be pressure on the side batting second to maintain the required run rate. It will thus be easier for the fielding captain to pressure the batting side. On the other hand, some teams prefer batting last because they then know how many runs they need to score to achieve victory.

If the pitch is wet, captains have to make a difficult choice. Some captains will bat first because the pitch will be in its best condition and there will be a chance of it taking a lot of spin as it dries out. On the other hand, some captains may put in the opposition, hoping to bowl them out cheaply in difficult conditions. The ball might keep low and skid in the wet; as it dries out the pitch may "take off", with the ball jumping disconcertingly. It is very difficult to score runs on wet pitches if the bowlers maintain a good line and length.

Batting order

The opening batsmen must have good technique to combat the opposition's new-ball bowlers and they must occupy the crease for sufficient time to give the team a good batting start.

Batsmen numbers three, four and five are the strokemakers of the side. They are ideally suited to batting when the ball is a little older and not moving as much as the new one. They look to play sensible, free-scoring shots and build an innings. It is important that the top six batsmen score the majority of the runs if a large total is required.

Batsman number six will be either another free-scoring player or, depending on the match situation, a dour player, hard to get out and used to scoring rather slowly. This type of batsman adds solidity to the team, particularly when early wickets have been lost.

If the wicketkeeper can bat, he may be best put in as number seven or eight where he can score consistent runs and from time to time make a couple of big scores. Some teams may be lucky in having an all-rounder in the team — a batsman who can bowl or vice versa. Again, he could occupy the number seven or eight spot.

The bowlers generally bat at eight, nine, 10 and 11. Although 10 and 11 usually don't score many runs, they may have to occupy the crease while one of the recognised batters is trying to score runs at the other end. Generally tailend batters are the big hitters of the team who like to hit sixes and fours.

Depending on the match situation, the captain may alter the batting order, perhaps promoting one of the big hitters when quick runs are required in the case of an early declaration or so the match can be won. Or perhaps the team has been fielding for five hours and is now going in to bat with an hour's batting time left. The openers will start the innings, but with the fall of a wicket and 20 minutes or so of play remaining the captain may decide to call on a "night-watchman" to bat. This is to protect the top order batsmen — the night-watchman's job is simply to stay in until stumps. The best equipped tailend batsman is usually given the job and is regarded as a sacrifice. While he may be easy prey for fast bowlers next morning, he has done his job the night before. Often the "nightie" likes the job because it gives him an opportunity to show the batsmen that he can bat and make a big score.

A sequence which illustrates a captain's role under pressure. The bowler is Australian spinner Bruce Yardley. I am the batsman. Graham Wood fielding close-in dives to take a possible bat/pad catch then sits looking at the umpire as the catch is disallowed. Keeper Rodney Marsh has appealed strongly. Yardley showed signs of displeasure, throwing his arms in the air, then flinging his sweater on the ground when he received it from umpire Mr Bricknell at the end of the over. In the final photograph captain Greg Chappell speaks quietly to Yardley out in the field, settling him down. From that point on Yardley got on with the game of cricket.

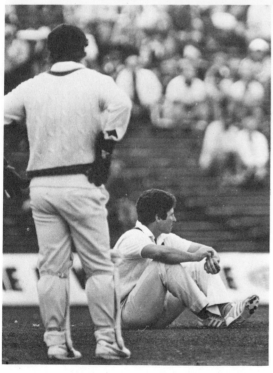

Bowling changes

A fast bowler should bowl for five or six overs in his opening session and then be given a spell by the third seam bowler in the side. He will bowl perhaps as many as 12 overs in a row. After an hour or so the fast bowler may be brought back into the attack for three or four fast overs and then spelled again. If a new batsman comes to the wicket, the captain may bring back his fast bowlers to unsettle the batsman and get him out.

Bowlers should be rotated, bowling shortish spells and with changes of ends. Ends can vary considerably: the breeze may differ, or there may be a slope at one end of the pitch that allows for more seam. If the pitch is turning early in the game get your spinner on.

Any bowler who starts to get hit around should be removed from the crease and re-placed. And don't let your bowlers get too tired. They could lose line and length and find it difficult to come back and bowl at a later stage. If you keep the fast bowlers reasonably fresh at all times by using them in short spells they will be more effective.

Field placement

The captain should liaise with his bowler before setting the field. With a new ball an attacking field should be set with, say, four slips, gully, fine leg, cover, mid-on, bat/pad or short square leg. The new ball will move in the air and off the seam, with a good chance of flying off the edge of the bat into the slips. Again, the new ball is very hard and with the extra bounce off the pitch it may fly off the edge of the bat or handle/glove into the bat/pad area.

As the ball becomes older and the batsmen

With the Australian pace attack on top, Greg Chappell has packed the slip cordon against New Zealand. Chappell, Border, Alderman and Hughes provide four slips while Yardley and Dyson crouch in the gully.

start to score more freely, the field will be set more defensively: say, two slips, gully, third man, fine leg, square leg, mid-on, mid-off and cover. If the outfield is fast and the pitch is fast the slips will stand finer, as will third man and fine leg; cover will be straighter and mid-on and mid-off straight. On the other hand, if the pitch is slow and the outfield has long grass making it slow as well, the positioning will be slightly different. The slips will stand wider because the ball coming off the edge of the bat will be a thick edge, coming into the slips at a wider angle. The third man and fine leg will be, say, 10 metres off the boundary edge because the ball will be travelling more slowly over the long grass. They will also position themselves at a wider angle, deflections and edges being thicker and wider.

The field above is for the medium pace or quick bowler who can move the ball away from the batsman. If the bowler can bowl an off-cutter or an inswinger with the new ball the field will be heavier on the leg side: for example, fine leg, leg slip or gully, square leg/mid-wicket, mid-on, and bat/pad. The off side may be two slips, backward point or gully and cover. As the ball gets older and doesn't move as much, there will be one slip, backward point, cover and mid-off; the on-side close catchers may be moved back into the circle of fielders, but still the emphasis will be on the leg side.

The captain should pressure an incoming batsman by having several fieldsmen in a catching position, trying to unsettle him and deprive him of that early single which will get him off the mark. When a batsman is in the 90s the field can also be brought in, to inhibit him reaching the magical 100.

With spin bowlers and a turning pitch field placings should be attacking. If the ball is turning to leg there may be six fielders on the leg side — leg slip, bat/pad, short mid-on, square leg, mid-wicket and mid-on. Three fielders will be on the off side — slip, wide cover and mid-off. Or you may decide to do without the slip, and move him to in front of point, or bring him into a catching position at silly mid-off. The line that the bowler should bowl is off

stump, forcing the batsman to play on the leg side.

When the ball is turning to off (that is, leg spin bowling) the off side field will be five men with four on the leg side. There will be slip, gully, point, cover, mid-off, mid-on, mid-wicket, square leg and perhaps a bat/pad close-in catcher. Obviously if spinners are being hit around the park, the close catchers will be moved back and a deep catcher will be positioned at wide mid-on close to the boundary. If some of the outfielders are positioned on the boundary it may persuade the batsman *not* to try hitting the ball to or over the boundary; he may play more cautiously, so close-in catchers could be deployed to seize on any close-in air shots.

The declaration

In some games declarations have to be made if a result is to be obtained. But the captain has to judge that declaration very well. He has both to give his team the best chance of winning and at the same time keep the opposition interested in chasing the runs if there is only a limited period of play remaining.

For example, Team A declares its second innings, leaving Team B 180 minutes to score 240 runs. In the time left, 60 overs will be bowled, so Team B will need to score at the rate of four runs per over.

The declaring captain must take the following into account.

Ø Will the runs be scored easily?

Ø Are all the bowlers fit enough and good enough to contain and get the opposition out during that period of time?

Ø What is the current run rate obtained during the game so far? If the current rate has been, say, three runs per over, you would give them at least four and perhaps four and a half runs per over.

Ø The state of the pitch. Will it deteriorate

further, making it hard to score the runs, let alone survive?

Ø The weather. Be careful here. If you declare too early because rain is forecast, and it doesn't rain, you will have given the opposition an easy target.

In a three-day game you may declare leaving the opposition all day to score, say, 320 runs. With this declaration you are backing your bowlers to win the game for you, because you have all day to bowl the other side out. Not very often would the batting side win the match from that position, so a win to you — or a draw — would be the result. If the game falls a little flat — you cannot get the batsmen out yet they are not interested in scoring the runs required — then you may well open the game up by using slow bowlers and giving the batsmen easy runs, to put them back into the game. That can be a risky tactic, but it is positive play and can pay dividends.

If both captains play the game negatively by batting on and on and on then the game becomes boring for both the players and the spectators. Declarations are an important part of the game for senior players. (Youngsters usually play one-innings games only.)

Discipline

Some players may need disciplining if they turn up late for training or for the start of a match, or if they argue with the umpires or get into verbal or physical clashes with the opposition. It is the captain's responsibility to see that these players are reprimanded in some way so that standards are kept. It happens only rarely, but in severe cases it may involve the player missing a match as a punishment. The coach or manager will be involved in this decision, but the captain should have some say.

At training or in a match the captain may decide to have a fining session for every misfield or dropped catch, or for those players that score nought. This sort of discipline is meant to be fun and should be treated that way. And it will certainly make the players try harder because they won't want to be embarrassed by having made a mistake. A 10 cent fine might be imposed — it could go into a team kitty to help pay for an end-of-season party.

Other responsibilities of the captain

WARM-UPS

Prior to the day's play the captain should ensure that every player has had a proper warm-up involving loosening up exercises and batting, bowling and fielding practice.

RECALLING THE BATSMAN

This is possibly a contentious issue, but the situation may arise. The umpire has given the batsman out, caught by the keeper. But the "snick" may have been off the pad and not the bat, or the ball may not have carried to the keeper on the full. The captain may wish to advise the umpire that a mistake has been made and for the decision to be reversed. But he must be very sure that a genuine mistake has been made.

FINAL TEAM SELECTION

Some captains may be asked to comment on various player selections. The captain must go onto the field with a happy side and one that he basically wants. If he has several players that don't respond to his "calls" then that can lead to a troubled and unsuccessful team.

The selectors may have picked 12 players in the squad with one to be omitted on the morning of the match. Conditions of the pitch will invariably influence the final decision. If the selectors have added an extra spin bowler to the side he will not play if the pitch is green, hard, fast and bouncy. If the pitch is bare of grass and looks like turning later in the game then the spinner may be selected and a seam bowler omitted.

The captain should help make the decision on the final selection and advise the non-player that he is 12th man — as well as let everyone know who is playing. It is his responsibility.

THE USE OF THE ROLLER BETWEEN INNINGS

The captain of the side coming to bat has the opportunity to have the use of the roller for seven minutes between innings. Always liaise with the groundsman on how the pitch plays in certain situations.

Generally speaking, a heavy roller should be used if the pitch is wet or soft. It will bring more moisture to the surface, making the pitch more placid until it starts to dry out — then it can be a little unpredictable. If the pitch is dry, however, the heavy roller could break the pitch by making it crumble. This would certainly help spin bowlers, so the batting captain would avoid using that roller. The light roller is often used on pitches to flatten any divots or pieces taken out of the pitch. This roller is often used when batting in the last innings.

TAKING THE NEW BALL

When 85 overs have been bowled there is an option to take a new ball. If the two batsmen have been in for some time and are dominating play, the new ball should be taken to try to get the breakthrough.

Often the scoring rate will pick up after the new ball is taken, because it is harder and travels more quickly. Semi-attacking fields should be set if both batsmen are in-form.

But if the pitch is turning, the batsmen are having difficulty in scoring and wickets are falling at regular intervals prior to the 85 overs, the new ball probably shouldn't be taken until much later, if at all.

APPEALING AGAINST THE LIGHT

If the light is bad the umpires will give the batting side a choice of whether to bat on or come off until the light improves. If the captain is not batting at the time and a decision has to be made, he should give his batsmen clear instructions. (In some cases the umpires may rule the game postponed.)

If the captain has to make a decision, he will consider the state of the game. If his team is struggling, then obviously he will welcome the chance of getting off the field of play as soon as possible. But if he is in a healthy position and wants to reinforce the advantage he possesses he may decide to bat on and take a chance.

Be careful, however. Once you come off the field of play because of bad light the umpires will not start play again until it improves. A lot of time may be lost and this could affect the outcome of the game.

FORFEITING AN INNINGS
(if regulations permit)

This happens very rarely and only when a two-innings game is badly affected by rain and the playing hours are greatly reduced. For example, Team A bats first and scores 250 for 6 when the rains come and one and a half of the three days are washed out. At the resumption of play, Team A declares. Team B forfeits its first innings, assuming that the follow-on is not enforced. Team A then forfeits its second innings, leaving Team B 251 runs to win in the final innings.

PLAYING IN WET CONDITIONS

The playing area and the surrounding outfield may be unfit for play and the umpires agree that play should be delayed until conditions improve. The umpires may ask the captains for their thoughts on starting. If both captains want to play and agree to start earlier, then the umpires may consider their wishes. If the captains don't agree, then the umpires will make the final decision. If the captains want to play, then they must consider the safety of their players. Slippery and treacherous conditions can cause unnecessary injury.

CHAPTER NINE

EQUIPMENT

Players should be neatly and correctly dressed. Boots should be clean and well spiked. Avoid wearing wristwatches or rings — watches may break, and being hit on a finger that has a ring could cause injury or even loss of that finger.

BAT

The selection of a suitable bat is of the utmost importance. It is far better for a player to have a bat that is a little light than one that is too heavy. The following tips on bat selection should be useful for young cricketers.

Length of bat	Length of handle	Width	Weight	Height of user	Age
Harrow 34"	11"	4¼"	2 lb 3oz	5'5"-5'7"	16+
Size 6 33"	10¾"	4"	2 lb	5'2"-5'5"	14-16
Size 5 31½"	10¾"	4"	2 lb	5'1"-5'2"	11-14
Size 4 30¼"	10½"	3⅞"	1 lb 8oz	4'77"-5'1"	8-10
Metric sizes					
Harrow 86.4cm	27.9cm	10.8cm	992g	1.65-1.70m	
Size 6 83.8cm	27.3cm	10.2cm	907g	1.57-1.65m	
Size 5 80.0cm	27.3cm	10.2cm	907g	1.55-1.57m	
Size 4 76.8cm	26.7cm	9.8cm	680g	1.40-1.55m	

POINTS TO CONSIDER

Ø If a full-size bat is selected, do you want a long handle or a short handle?

Ø Left or right-handed bat? The difference is the shape and angle of the toe of the bat. One side of the end is more rounded to assist the batsman sliding his bat into the batting crease.

Ø The grip — thick or thin? You may require another rubber grip on the handle.

Ø The weight and balance of the bat must feel comfortable when it is picked up.

Ø The bat should be well oiled if it does not have a polyplastic or nylon protective cover.

Ø To keep it clean use sandpaper on a normal bat, but on a polyplastic covered bat a damp rag is enough to remove dirt and ball marks.

PADS

They should fit comfortably on the legs and offer solid protection particularly across the knee and down the middle of each leg. They should not be too cumbersome or heavy, nor prevent quick movement of the feet and easy running between the wickets.

Select pads according to right or left-handedness. The actual side wing of the front leg pad is vital for protection around the calf muscle area. A left-hand batsman should *not* use right-hand pads because that protective side wing would be on the wrong side.

ABDOMINAL PROTECTOR (BOX)

These should always be worn when batting at practice or in a match. A wicketkeeper should always use one as well. A nasty knock in that area is painful and sickening, so take the precaution. There are two types available — one that slips inside an athletic support, and a strap-on type that is tied around the waist and between the legs.

THIGH PAD

These are recommended for use against fast bowlers. To be hit on the leg without this protection can cause bruising and could slow your movements down when batting, running between the wickets and fielding. Again, it should be comfortable and not be restricting.

BATTING GLOVES

Wear gloves at all times when batting, even when having throw-downs. They will help you grip the bat handle and give you added confidence. Again, choose gloves suitable for your requirements. The thumb protector, for example, differs for right and left-hand batsmen. The fingers and back of the hand should be well protected and the palm should have a leather face.

BOOTS

No bowler can perform efficiently and effectively if he has trouble with his feet. Bowlers should have lightweight leather boots with high ankle supports to prevent the twisting of an ankle in delivery and to prevent foot movement inside the boot. Screw-in or built-in spikes should be long so that you do not slip and slide when running in to bowl and at delivery. A drag plate may be necessary on the boot you drag with at delivery to save the toe of the boot from wearing through.

Batting and fielding boots may differ. Many players prefer a lighter boot for fielding with a cut-away ankle support. Often the soles are nylon or rubber. Make sure you have good arch supports in the boots to prevent pressure points on the ankle. Bat in spiked boots unless the pitch is in such good condition that it allows you to use rubber-soled shoes.

CARE OF THE FEET

To help prevent blisters a good thick pair of woollen socks should be worn — some bowlers will wear two pairs. An inner sole may be also necessary to help comfort. Foot powder will make them feel fresh and prevent tinea, and vaseline between the toes will help prevent blisters.

If the bottom of your feet are relatively soft use methylated spirits to harden them. This is particularly helpful for bowlers. Bruised heels are a common bowler's complaint; the use of sponge rubber could solve the problem.

CRICKET CLOTHES

Polyester/cotton cricket shirts are probably the best. They are thick and warm and absorb perspiration. On cold days a singlet should be worn and on hot days it may also be advisable for bowlers to wear one in order to soak up perspiration, thus helping to prevent chills in the back after finishing a bowling spell. Bowlers can bowl in a short-sleeved jersey but not in a long-sleeved one — it restricts body movement far too much.

Trousers should fit comfortably — not too baggy in the seat, not too loose around the waist, not too long in the leg (just over the first three or four eyelets of the boots is ideal).

Caps will prevent glare on bright sunny days. Floppy hats are often worn by fielders to help prevent sunburn around the neck. I don't recommend batting in floppy hats in windy conditions because they tend to blow off the head and could fall on the wicket and cause your dismissal.

HELMETS

These are now becoming an accepted part of protective equipment. I am a firm believer that they should be worn when pitch conditions are bad and when facing fast bowlers. It not only gives the batsman more confidence to get in behind the line of the ball but also could be literally a life-saver.

Close-in fielders should also wear helmets, particularly at the bat/pad position. Parents and coaches should stress player safety and advise accordingly.

MEDICAL KIT

In my gear I carry a medical kit that will help me get through a day's play: bandages, tape, lip cream, sunburn cream, massage cream, skin cream, glue, knife, screw driver, scissors, spare sprigs, spare laces, sponge rubber, inner soles, cotton wool, tinea and talcum powder, sprig tightener, chewing gum, needle and cotton, disprin, sandpaper and bat oil.

THE BALL

A 156-gram (5½-ounce) four-piece, leather, cork and rubber centred ball is recommended, although two-piece balls are used in some grades. At the beginning of the innings, a fast bowler may be able to select a new ball to be played with. In making his choice he should look for the following points:

Ø A high seam to allow the ball to move off the pitch.

Ø A dark colour — for some reason darker balls swing more than lighter ones.

Ø The ball must feel comfortable in the hand. All balls feel different, so select the one that fits nicely in the fingers and is not too greasy. A greasy ball will slip out of the hand and will be thus harder to control.

Ø Some balls differ in shape and appear to be slightly bigger than others. A small ball is desirable, because it is easier to grip and the fingers can control it easier.

WICKETKEEPING GEAR

Careful selection of wicketkeeping gloves and inner gloves is essential. Gloves should have supple leather and fit comfortably.

Pads are also important. Some wicketkeepers wear a pair of pads that come up to the knee only, instead of the usual batting pads. This helps quicken their movement behind the stumps because the pads are lighter and not as bulky.

UMPIRE'S COUNTER

An effective ball counter is needed to count the balls bowled in the over. Match sticks, coins, pebbles and so on can do the job. Do not count balls bowled on your fingers.

CHAPTER TEN

CRICKET GAMES TO DEVELOP SKILLS

This chapter is designed to assist you in developing your game by practising by yourself or with other players. It is important to achieve maximum benefits from training. If you decide to practise, it is far better to work hard for 60 minutes than to fool around, talking about other things than cricket and generally wasting time for two hours.

Batting

Ø Practising shots in front of a mirror is terrifically helpful. By looking in the mirror you can see if you have picked the bat up and brought it down correctly. Practise correct body positioning — standing side on, head straight and still, eyes level looking over your front shoulder, the grip and so on.

Ø The ball is placed on a tee and hit to a target. A rubber tee is recommended. Address the ball in the normal way and stroke the ball to or through the various targets. You should be able to practise most shots.

Ø Net practice is probably the best way to practise because it most closely approximates a match situation. Try to "stay in" during your time at the nets and experiment with new techniques and shots, something you cannot afford to do in a match. It helps to have different types of bowlers bowling at you in the nets, say two fast bowlers and a spinner. This quick-changing variety will help improve concentration.

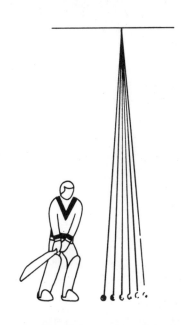

A simple way to practise batting skills. The ball is suspended in a sock or bag.

Ø Hang a ball in a sock or bag, tie a piece of string on to it and hang it from the garage roof or clothes line. The ball should be around 10 centimetres off the ground. You can play this practice rig as either a stationary or a moving ball — play shots accordingly. Make sure that you are always behind the line of the ball.

Ø Practise batting with a golf ball and a wicket. Have someone bowl or throw the ball at your bat, the theory being that if you can hit a golf ball consistently well you must be able to hit a cricket ball even better with a cricket bat.

Group batting skills. Fielders can be placed in a large circle around the batsman for the sweep, drive, cut and so on.

Batting skills. The coach drops the ball which is hit to the fielders.

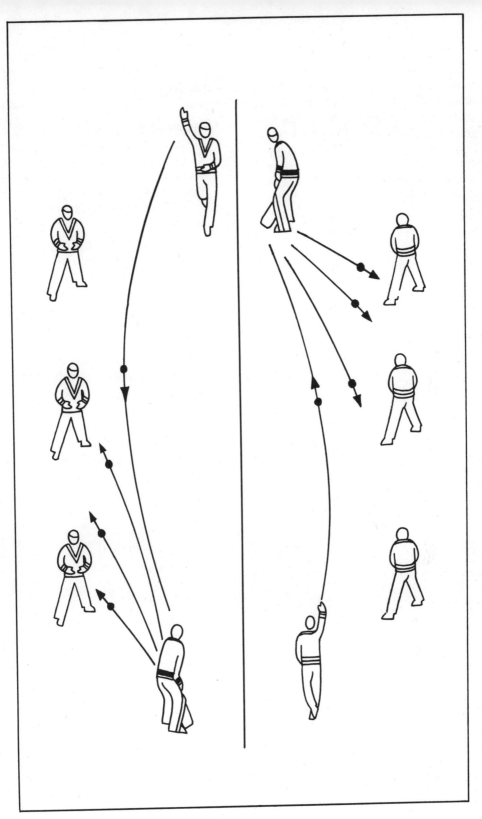

Two different groups practising on-driving in a confined area.

Ø Hitting a dropped ball to target or fielders. Another variation is for the ball to be bowled or thrown underarm. The ball must bounce on a good length so that the batsman can hit it properly. The bowler is *not* trying to get the batsman out but is giving him practice timing the ball and hitting it in various directions. After the batsman has hit, say, 20 balls, move around a position so that everyone bats, bowls, keeps and fields.

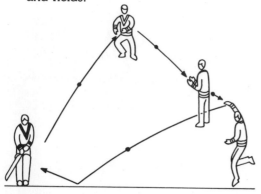

Group batting practice. The ball is hit to the fielder at mid-wicket who returns it to mid-on and then to the bowler.

Bowling

Ø As with batting, you can usefully practise your action at delivery facing a mirror. Correct your action so that you are in fact looking over your front shoulder, you have your front arm high, body side on and bowling arm going high and coming down straight.

Ø Bowling at one stump. If you can hit one wicket at practice you should be able to hit three wickets in a game. It pays to put a marker down on a good length; about 3 metres in front of the batting crease is a good start.

Ø Bowling to a partner and having a competition to see who gets the most wickets. A wicket is placed at both ends.

Ø Bowl with a golf ball, aiming to hit a wicket set up in front of a brick wall. The ball will rebound off the wall and on your follow-through you have to stop it or catch it. This will help your reflexes and agility in the field.

Practising bowling skills in pairs. The correct bowling length can be marked on the ground.

Ø When bowling in the nets you should try to assess the batsman's weaknesses and bowl to them. Practise your match rhythm and timing — do not change your style or run-in. Award yourself points over, say, 12 balls. Give yourself three points for a ball that pitches on middle and off stump and is played defensively or gets the batsman out; two points if the ball is pitched on or outside off stump and no runs are scored; one point if it is wide of the off stump or if you think the batsman has scored a run; and no points for anything down the leg side. Of a possible 36 points, any score over 24 is very good, 18–24 satisfactory. Any score under 18 means that you have a lot of hard work to do.

Net practice. One reserve batsman to each net padding up, three bowlers to each net, the coach supervising.

Catching

CLOSE TO WICKET CATCHING

Ø Using a roller. The ball is thrown onto the roller to come off at different angles.

Ø A throws the ball underarm to B, the batsman, who edges the ball into the awaiting slips fielders, C.

Ø A slip cradle really tests your reflexes and catching ability. It consists of wooden slats nailed on a slope so that when the ball is thrown into the cradle, it speeds off in different angles into the slips area.

Ø "Piggy in the middle." Form a circle of, say, nine fielders and have one person placed in the middle. The ball is thrown by the outfielders to the player in the middle who has to catch, say, 20. When he has achieved that number, someone else takes a turn in the middle and does the same. Continue until everyone has had a go. Make sure that the person in the middle is worked hard and that he has to dive to take some catches. Throw just out of his normal standing reach.

Catching skills with a roller.

Slip catching skills.

Using a slip cradle.

"Piggy in the middle."

General catching practice in pairs.

"Touch rugby."

Catching practice — the fielder in front must catch ten. If he misses, the other fielders catch or stop the ball.

General fielding skills. The coach throws the ball into the gaps.

Ø General catching practice can be done as illustrated. Just throw the ball underarm to an opponent who has to catch the ball. Have a competition — the first to catch, say, 20.

Ø *"Touch rugby."* Make up two teams of five players. The object is to score between the goals at each end and players must throw the ball to team-mates before being touched by the opposition. If a player is touched in possession of the ball, or he drops the ball, the other side gets possession. This is a fast moving game and is ideal to start a practice with.

Ø *Formation catching.* Form two lines, say of four in each line. Line A is the front line and line B is the back line, with the fielders placed in the gaps. The batsman hits the ball in the gaps or to the fielders. The object here is to get the players to call for the ball if two are in a position to catch it, thus improving team work and understanding.

Throwing

Ø Form a circle with a wicket placed at the centre. Throw the ball at the stump to hit it. The first player to hit it 10 times wins.

Ø Form two teams and line up on opposite sides of a wicket, about 20 metres away. One players starts by throwing the ball at the wicket and each player in turn runs in towards the ball the opposition has thrown. When throws have missed the wicket, run in, pick the ball up and throw at the wicket. This must be done as quickly as possible. This is a pressure situation of the type that can occur in a match when trying to run out a batsman. The first team to knock the wickets over 15 times is the winner. The fielder must pick the ball up and throw no closer than 15 metres from the wickets.

You can practise this by yourself by placing a wicket in front of a brick wall.

Throw a golf/tennis/rubber ball at the wicket from varying distances. If you miss, the ball will bounce back; run in towards it, pick up and throw.

Ø Another method of practising throwing for accuracy. Throw a rubber/tennis ball against a brick wall and try to hit the circles that have been painted on the wall. Start from a very close distance and increase the length of the throw once you have mastered it. It is important for those fielders that are positioned on the boundary to have an accurate throw of some 60–70 metres.

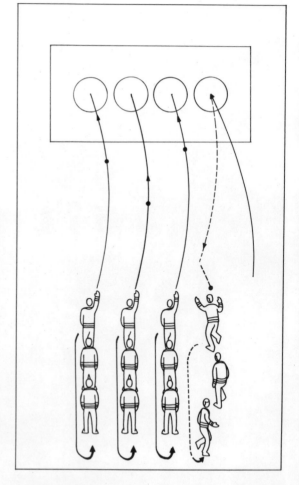

Practising throwing accuracy against a wall.

RUNNING, RETRIEVING, PICKING UP, THROWING (repeated)

This is a speed work exercise.

Four balls are placed at regular intervals. The runner sprints to the first ball, picks it up and throws it back to the catcher. The runner runs back to the start and then sprints out to the second ball and throws that back. He repeats the exercise until all the balls have been collected.

Another: the wicketkeeper rolls the ball out 20-30 metres. The fielder sprints after the ball, picks it up, turns and throws back to the keeper. On his way back to join the group the keeper may give him a catch or another ball to pick up and underarm back. This can involve all the fielders and demands that the wicketkeeper position himself correctly over the stumps. If the returns are not very good, make the fielder do the routine again until he has improved.

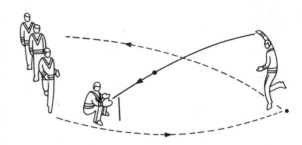

Retrieving practice. The fielder chases the ball thrown by the keeper and returns it at speed.

Fielding skills. A relay involving running, retrieving, picking up and throwing.

Running between wickets

This can be a lot of fun. Form two teams of, say, six players. One team bats or does the running, while the other team does the fielding. The object of the exercise is for the fielding team to run the batsman out before he completes his run.

A throws the ball out so that B, the fielder, has to run after it. He retrieves and returns the ball to the keeper while C, the batsman, is trying to complete two runs. When the batting side is all out, change over. The new batting side has to score more runs to win. The batsman has to sprint 20–30 metres and slide his bat into the crease while the fielders must move in quickly towards the ball and get it back to the keeper accurately and quickly.

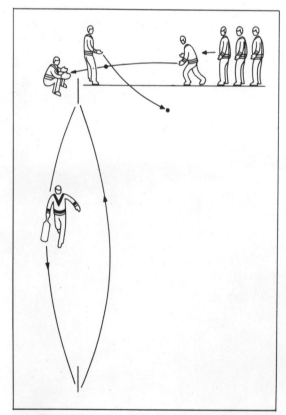

Practising running between wickets in teams. The batsman has to run two while the fielder returns the ball.

Wicketkeeping

The wicketkeeper should be involved in as many of the fielding routines as possible.

Ø Have someone hit balls to the keeper from, say, 10 metres. The ball must be hit very firmly so that he has to move quickly into position and even dive if necessary.

Ø Have a specialist bowler bowl at a wicket and make the keeper practise rising with the ball and taking it cleanly waist high.

Ø Position a batsman in front of the wicket and bowl to him. Have him deliberately miss a ball from time to time to test the keeper. (Remember, not every ball goes through to the keeper in a match.)

Cricket games

Many young cricketers are not quite ready to play in normal 11-a-side matches. Whilst one or two players may have a sound basic understanding of the game they usually dominate various games with the result that many youngsters become bystanders and are not involved in the game. They may lose interest and eventually give the game away. All young cricketers should be given equal opportunities and be totally involved in some aspect of the game.

NON-STOP OR CONTINUOUS CRICKET

Two equal teams are selected. Equipment includes one bat, a set of wickets or a rubbish bin used as the wickets; two skittles or markers positioned 8–10 metres from the wicket at right angles, and a tennis, rubber or cricket ball. The game can be played in a gym, hall or outside.

A batsman stands at the wicket to take strike. The bowler bowls from a standing position underarm about 8–15 metres from the batsman. The ball must reach the batsman on the bounce and is not bowled too fast. When the batsman has hit the ball, he must run to the skittles or markers positioned to his left or right and back again to take strike.

A fieldsman gathers the ball and returns it to the bowler as soon as possible. When the bowler has the ball, he can bowl whether the batsman is ready or not, although the bowler must be in the correct position. If the bowler hits the wickets the batsman is out. But if he misses, the wicketkeeper throws the ball to the bowler who tries again. The batsman can be out caught in the normal way or, if played in a gym, he can be caught off the wall or ceiling. No matter how the batsman is out, the incoming batsman must get into position quickly, because the bowler can keep bowling.

This is a fast and exciting game for youngsters, allowing for good fast running between the wickets, alertness and expert fielding and hitting.

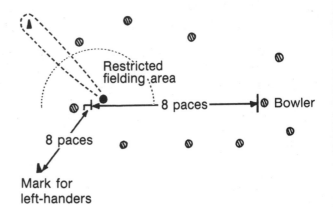

Non-stop or continuous cricket. The dotted circle keeps fielders at a reasonable distance.

Continuous cricket.

MULTI-CONTINUOUS CRICKET

This is a continuation of non-stop cricket with a drum used as the wicket and four single stumps positioned about 15 metres from the drum in a circle. The ball is returned by any fielder to one of the four bowlers positioned behind the stumps. As soon as a bowler has the ball he may bowl, whether the batsman has made his crease or not. The same rules apply as before. This game is more suited to larger groups.

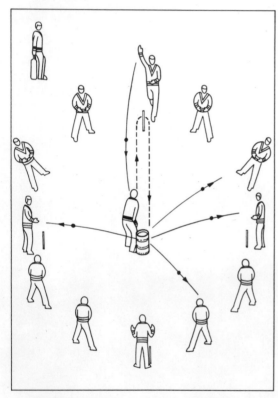

Multi-continuous cricket. The ball can be bowled from four different positions each marked by a stump.

ROTATION CRICKET

A batsman bats for an allocated number of balls. The wicketkeeper and fielders are in their normal positions. The next batsman is at square leg safely padding up. At the end of the batsman's time he takes over the wicket-

keeping, while the former keeper moves around to square leg to remove his pads.

All fielders move round a position in a clockwise direction, except first slip, who starts to pad up.

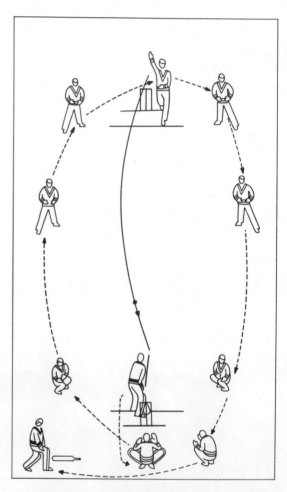

Rotation cricket. The incoming batsman has come from first slip. At the end of the practice every player has been involved in batting, bowling, fielding and wicketkeeping.

SIX AND EIGHT-ASIDE CRICKET (indoor)

This game can be played in a good-sized gym or hall with a tennis ball. There are six or eight players in each team and the pitch is full size or smaller depending on the size of the room.

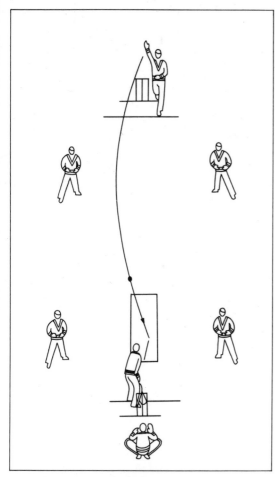

Six and eight-a-side cricket in an enclosed space such as a gym or hall. If the ball does not pitch in the area marked on the floor a wide is called.

The batsman can be out in the normal way plus being caught off the walls, and is also out if the ball hits the ceiling or the wall behind him on the full. If he hits the walls with the ball going along the ground he is credited with two runs. He can also run singles. If he manages to hit the wall behind the bowler along the ground four runs are scored; he scores six runs if he hits the wall on the full. He cannot be out if he hits six. Only one batsman bats at a time and when he is out a new batsman takes over. If the batsman fails to score off six consecutive fair deliveries, playing out a maiden, he is out.

At least three bowlers must be used, unless the batting side is out before all three have bowled. Should a wicket fall in his over, the bowler can start again. If time is short the batsman can be restricted to a maximum amount of overs.

A bowling target should be drawn on the floor, in line with the leg stump and on a slightly over-pitched length. A suggested size for average bowlers could be 60 centimetres wide and 2 metres long. If the bowler misses this target the umpire awards a wide. Wides, byes and leg byes all count to the batsman's score.

EIGHT-AND-UNDER CRICKET

Many young players around seven or eight years of age take to playing cricket in the under-10 division, often because there is no opportunity for them to play in their own age group. It would be preferable to organise a junior team for them because the difference in age and skill when playing against older cricketers can make them afraid of the ball and force them onto the back foot when batting.

It is suggested to any coach organising an under-eight game that bowling not be left to the youngsters and that the ball be delivered by the coach. This will avoid wasting time, which would happen if a bowler of this age was asked to bowl. The coach can bowl under-arm consistently to a marked area so that the young batsmen are encouraged to move into the ball without fear.

Restrictions may have to be made in field placings to allow runs to be scored in front of the wicket, and boundaries may have to be reduced.

STOOL BALL

Make up three groups of four players into teams A, B and C. One group will bat, one will bowl and field close to the bat. The other team supplies the outfield.

The pitch is normal size if possible, and the wickets are stools or chairs or stands and

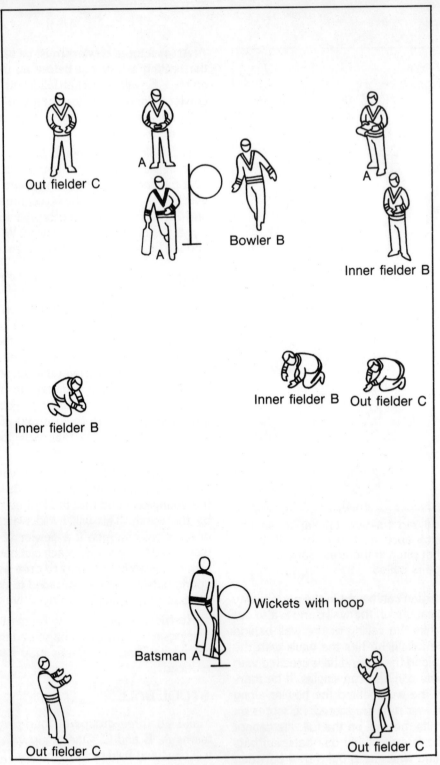

Out fielder C

A

A

Bowler B

A

Inner fielder B

Inner fielder B

Inner fielder B   Out fielder C

Wickets with hoop

Batsman A

Out fielder C

Out fielder C

Stool ball. The players are divided into three teams of four players. The ball is bowled underarm and the batsman must touch the wicket with his bat. The batting side provides a scorer and an umpire.

hoops. The bowler bowls from midway between the wickets and bowls underarm. A six-ball over is bowled. At the completion of that over the new bowler bowls at the alternate wickets.

Runs are scored in the normal way, but the batsman must touch the wicket with his bat to make his ground; otherwise he is run out. He can also be out caught or bowled (if the ball goes through the hoop or hits the stool/wickets). If the batsman cannot reach the ball, a wide is called, one run is added to the total and an extra ball has to be bowled.

Team A bats with two batsmen at a time until all four players have been dismissed or the maximum number of batting overs have been completed. Team B bowls and provides three fielders in the inner ring. Each player will bowl an over before the same bowler can bowl two overs.

Team C will provide the four fielders in the outer ring fielding in the deep, two on the leg side and two on the off. While the batting side is in the two batsmen not batting will keep score and umpire.

At the completion of the innings, the batting team becomes the outfielding team, the bowling team bats and the outfielders become the infielders and the bowling team. The team with the highest score wins.

PAIRS CRICKET

This can be played indoors or out, depending on the room available. It involves 12 players in six pairs. Two bats and a tennis or rubber ball are needed for indoor play, or a cricket ball for outdoors (in which case pads and other protective equipment will also be necessary).

A work card is needed to keep the scores and to show where each pair should be positioned during the game — each pair is playing against the other five pairs. Each pair will bat for, say, four overs — whether they get out during that period or not. At the conclusion of their innings their score is divided by the number of times out, to get an average score. The winning pair will be the one with the highest average.

The normal rules of cricket apply, with the pairs rotating into a new position after each innings.

EIGHT-A-SIDE OUTDOOR CRICKET FOR SCHOOLBOYS

It is suggested that this game is played for 12 overs each side, which will take about 60–75 minutes. If 45 minutes or less is available the match could perhaps be spread over two games periods. Before the match commences the players of each team are allotted a number.

The fielding side provides a wicketkeeper and seven fielders, four of whom each bowl three overs. A double change of bowlers takes place at the end of the sixth over. The batting side provides two fieldsmen in addition to batting. These fieldsmen are not permitted to bowl or keep wicket while their side is batting.

If two independent umpires are not available, the batting side provides two umpires, two fieldsmen and two batsmen with two batsmen padded up. Batsmen can give unlimited chances, but each chance is recorded on the score sheet as a wicket lost.

The team scoring the highest average number of runs per wicket lost wins the match. The coach keeps score at the bowler's end and can give advice to the players.

ELEVEN-A-SIDE CRICKET

This is the normal type of cricket played. It can be as a one-day limited-over game, a three-day first class match or a five-day test match with each team having two innings. In a limited-over match the team with the highest score wins. In two, three or five-day matches the side with the higher aggregate in the two innings wins. Draws can result if the weather prevents the teams from completing their innings or if the innings of the team batting last is incomplete (that is, they are not all out or they have not overtaken the aggregate score of the other team). The captain can terminate his innings by making a declaration.

CHAPTER ELEVEN

UMPIRING

Good judgement, fair interpretation of the law, the ability to handle players' frustrations and decide on doubtful conditions and unfair play, and the possession of a high level of concentration are the necessary qualities of a good umpire. He must be decisive, firm and positive with decisions. If he makes a mistake — and this will happen — he must be brave enough to admit it and, if possible, change the decision.

Umpiring fundamentals

⊘ Before the toss, acquaint yourself with any special regulations. Some competitions may require special rules.

⊘ Discuss with both captains any conditions that will affect the conduct of the match, and agree on one watch or clock to be followed during play.

⊘ Umpires are the *sole* judges of unfair and fair play. They are also responsible for final decisions about the fitness of the ground for play.

⊘ In the event of the decision being left to them, umpires will decide if the weather and light is fit for play.

⊘ All disputes shall be determined by the umpires. If they disagree, the present state of play will continue.

⊘ Umpires will change ends at the conclusion of both teams' first innings.

⊘ When a signal is made, a call is given to inform the players and scorer.

⊘ The ball should be replaced by another ball with similar usage if it goes out of shape. It should weigh not less than 155.9 grams (5½ ounces) or more than 163 grams (5¾ ounces). It shall measure not less than 216 millimetres (8½ inches) or more than 229 millimetres (9 inches) in circumference.

⊘ Bats may be held to be checked to ensure their width is correct. A bat should not exceed 114 millimetres (4½ inches) at its widest point and not exceed 965 millimetres (38 inches) in length.

⊘ Check the pitch is 3.05 metres (10 feet) in width and a maximum of 20.12 metres (22 yards) long.

⊘ The three stumps should be 229 millimetres (9 inches) apart in total, and 711 millimetres (28 inches) high (for senior matches — they may be smaller for children's games).

⊘ The popping and bowling crease should be well marked. The bowling crease is 2.6 metres (8 feet 8 inches) in length and the return crease is 1.22 metres (4 feet). The popping crease is a minimum of 3.66 metres (12 feet).

⊘ Seven minutes only is allowed for a pitch to be rolled between innings.

⊘ If it rains, a pitch may be covered unless "special" regulations prevent this. Check to see that adequate covering is at the ground.

⊘ An "over" is called after six fair deliveries have been bowled (or eight deliveries, depending on "special regulations").

Equipment

A certain amount of equipment should be carried by umpires. It includes: a ball counter; pencil and paper to mark off the overs that a bowler has bowled if he is restricted to a maximum in the case of a one-day competition; sticking plaster in case someone receives a cut; a tape measure to see that the pitch markings and height of wickets are correct; a spare set of bails, often heavier ones in case a strong wind is blowing lighter bails off; a knife to cut loose threads off the ball, to cut tape and to remove dirt from the bottom of boots.

A selection of spare balls should be available in case replacement balls are needed (this is really the responsibility of the local club, but the umpire should see that they are available).

An umpire should carry a marker for the bowler. It is usually a round metal disc that the bowler places at the end of his run-up. Bowlers should use markers instead of scuffing the grass to make a mark.

Umpire's signals

Ø *Bye* — A run obtained from a ball untouched by the batsman's bat or body.

Ø *Leg bye* — A run from a ball untouched by the bat but hitting the batsman on the body.

Ø *Wide ball* — A ball delivered so high, or so wide of the wicket, that it passes out of the reach of the batsman standing in his normal position. A wide is called as soon as the ball passes the batsman.

Ø *No ball* — Some of the reasons for no balling are as follows: if the ball has been thrown by the bowler; if more than two men are fielding behind square leg at the time of delivery; if the bowler's front foot is not behind the bowling crease, or if the

bowler's back foot cuts or touches the return crease.

Ø *One short* — Called if the batsman, when running between the wickets, does not ground his bat or have his body pass the batting crease when turning for a second or third run.

Ø *Boundary four* — The ball passing over the boundary line after having bounced inside the line.

Ø *Boundary six* — The ball passing over the boundary on the full.

Ø *Dead ball* — If, in the opinion of the umpire, a batsman has not played a genuine shot at the ball and runs are obtained after the ball hits the batsman's body. No runs are given and the batsmen return to their respective ends.

Ø *Cancel previous decision* — A signal cancelling the previous one. The umpire has made a mistake and will signal again correctly.

Ø *Out* — A batsman can be given out 10 different ways:

— *Bowled* — when the wicket is broken from a bowler's fair delivery, or if the batsman hits the ball onto his wicket.

— *Caught* — a fair catch, held by a fielder before the ball touches the ground.

— *Run out* — if either batsman is found to be out of his ground and the wicket is broken. However, if the batsmen are running two, resulting from, say, an overthrow that has "broken" the wicket, the batsman can only be given run out at that end, if the fielder has the ball and a stump pulled out of the ground and held in the same hand or together.

— *Hit wicket* — if the batsman plays at the ball and accidentally hits the wicket with his body, cap/helmet or bat.

— *Handled ball* — if either batsman handles the ball while in play he can be given out upon an appeal from the opposition.

Dead ball.

One short.

Wide ball.

Boundary four.

Out.

Boundary six.

Cancel previous signal.

No ball.

Dickie Bird, the famous English umpire, demonstrates the umpire's signals.

- *Stumped* — the wicketkeeper can stump a batsman if the batsman is out of his crease while attempting to play at the ball.
- *Obstructing the field* — if a batsman willfully obstructs a fielder while attempting to catch a ball, he can be out upon appeal.
- *Timed out* — if the incoming batsman takes more than two minutes to reach the field of play (not the batting crease), the opposing side can appeal. Ideally, both batsmen should cross on the field of play.
- *Lbw* — the batsman is out lbw when hit on the pad or body, by a ball in line from wicket to wicket and which, in the umpire's opinion, would have hit the batsman's wicket. If the batsman makes no attempt to play at the ball and the ball pitches outside the off stump and would have hit the wickets, he can be adjudged out lbw as well. If the ball pitches outside the leg stump and the batsman has played no shot at it and the ball hits the batsman's body, he can also be adjudged lbw, provided the bowler has delivered the ball the opposite side of the batsman's wicket. An example: a right-arm bowler must bowl over the wicket to a right-hand batsman, or a left-hand bowler must bowl around the wicket to a right-hand batsman. To a left-hand batsman the right-arm bowler must bowl around the wicket and the left-arm bowler must bowl over the wicket.
- *Hit twice* — if the batsman hits the ball twice he can be given out. If defending his wicket, however, he can use his bat to stop the ball hitting the stumps.
- *Retired out* — a batsman can retire hurt and continue his innings at a later stage. However, if he leaves the field and does not wish to continue his innings he is retired out. One example: a batsman is given not out upon appeal and then decides to walk, knowing that a catch has been fairly taken. The umpire is entitled to give the batsman out retired out rather than to say "caught Marsh, bowled Lillee".

CHAPTER TWELVE

HOW TO SCORE

At some stage during a game you may be asked to score. Look at the scorebook entry here.

The match is between Canterbury and Auckland. It is Canterbury's first innings.

The batting order is recorded as the batsmen come out to bat and the bowling order as the bowlers come in to bowl.

Cunis bowls the first ball of the match. A dot signifies that no run is scored.

In fact no runs are scored off the first five balls, but off the sixth ball two runs are scored by the number one batsman, Bolton. He is credited with the runs. At the end of the over the total of runs scored off the over is marked, in this case two.

In addition, the overall score is marked off. Each run is marked on the running tally.

In Cunis' second over he bowls a no ball on the third ball. This is indicated by a circled dot. If the batsman has scored no runs off the bat off this ball, one run is credited to the total and also recorded in the extras column. But if Bolton scored two runs from the no ball he would be credited with those runs. Two runs would be recorded in the bowler's over with a circle round them. The extras column would not record the no ball because the batsman would have benefited from it.

In Sutton's second over his third ball was a wide. The dot is surrounded by a square and the run is recorded in the extras column, as well as being added to the total.

Sutton's third over was a maiden; i.e., no runs were scored off the bat during the over. At the completion of a maiden over, an "M" is written into the dots.

In the fifth ball of Sutton's fourth over he

has D'Arcy out, caught by the wicket-keeper Harford. In the bowler's over column the wicket is marked with an "x". In the "How out" column the scorer enters what has happened: "Caught Harford, bowled Sutton". The batsman's score is 7. A mark at the end of the scoring strokes column signifies the end of the innings.

Howarth's first over was a wicket maiden: no runs were scored and a wicket was taken. Hastings was out stumped Harford for 2 and the incoming batsman failed to score from the remaining ball. A "W" signifies the wicket maiden.

When a wicket falls the total score at that time is recorded in the "Fall of wicket" column. In this innings the first wicket fell at 16, the second at 20, the third at 22.

If the umpires signal a bye or leg bye the runs scored off that decision are recorded in the extras column.

At the completion of the innings the bowling total of 18 runs and eight extras comes to 26, as does the batting total of 18 runs and eight extras. It pays to check regularly to make sure that the batting and bowling all add up.

At the end of the innings the bowler's analysis is recorded. Here Sutton bowled four overs, including one maiden, conceded four runs and took one wicket. He bowled one wide.

When the number of runs hit off a bowler is marked at the end of each over it is added to those scored in previous overs.

When a bowler has finished his bowling spell, a thick line is drawn at the end of his last over. Here both Cunis and Sutton bowled four-over spells.

TEAM CANTERBURY   **V** AUCKLAND   **AT** AUCKLAND
INNINGS FIRST   **DATE** 24.3.65

	BATSMEN	HOW OUT	BOWLER	TOTAL
1	BOLTON 2133/.	BOWLED	WILLIAMS	9
2	D'ARCY 1221/.	c HARFORD	SUTTON	7
3	HASTINGS 2/.	st. HARFORD	HOWARTH	2
4	HARRIS	NOT OUT		0
5	HORTON	NOT OUT		0
6	CHAPPLE			
7	WARD			
8	MOTZ			
9	BARTLETT			
10	TAYLOR			
11	WALKER			

WIDES /   1
BYES
L. BYES 3/2   3
NO BALLS /   1
FALL OF WICKETS: 1 — 16   2 — 20   3 — 22

TOTAL FOR 3 WKTS   26

UMPIRES...
SCORERS...
PLAY COMMENCED .... STUMPS DRAWN
RESULT

BOWLERS	OVERS	MAIDENS	NO BALLS	WIDES	BALLS BOWLED	RUNS	WICKETS	RUNS PER WICKET
CUNIS	4	0	1	0	24	12	0	—
SUTTON	4	1	0	1	24	4	1	4
WILLIAMS	1	0	0	0	6	2	1	3
HOWARTH	1	1	0	0	5	0	1	5

CHAPTER THIRTEEN

A QUESTIONNAIRE

The following is a list of questions that you should answer to prove that you are fully conversant with the technicalities of the game. If you have read the book carefully you should score highly.

A guideline: 90 to 100 points is excellent, 70 to 89 is only satisfactory, and if you score under 70 then you should read the book again.

QUESTIONS

1. Name six important attitudes required by players if they want to have a better chance of being successful in the game of cricket (half point for each named). 3 points
2. Name three things that will help your concentration level when batting. 3 points
3. Fitness prevents and delays injury. What else will fitness do for a player? 2 points
4. Name six different types of exercises a bowler can do to prepare himself prior to the commencement of the day's play (half point for each type named). 3 points
5. Explain the theory of swing bowling. 3 points
6. If you were bowling to a tall batsman on a good batting pitch, what length would you try to bowl to him? 1 point
7. What does the word "length" mean, and how many different lengths are there? Name the lengths. 5 points
8. What field would you set to a right-handed batsman who has scored 60, and the bowler is a right-handed medium-pacer bowling with an old ball? What line would the bowler be bowling at and why? 5 points
9. If you are a fast new-ball bowler, what factors would you consider in choosing the right end to bowl from? 3 points
10. Explain the right grip for an outswing bowler. 3 points
11. If a fast bowler's front arm does not get very high at delivery what will happen to this bowler? 3 points
12. Explain the position of the batsman's hands on the bat. 3 points
13. In selecting a bat of your choice, what factors would you consider? 3 points
14. Name three methods of stopping a ball in the outfield. 3 points
15. If you lose concentration in the field, what can happen? 3 points
16. Name six qualities a wicketkeeper needs to be effective behind the stumps (half point for each quality named). 3 points
17. When running between the wickets, what are the three calls? 3 points

18. Name three other things a batsman should do when running between the wickets. 3 points

19. The umpire may have to make 10 signals at some stage during the game. Name them (half point each). 5 points

20. How many ways can a batsman be dismissed and name them. 10 points

21. If you are the captain of your team and won the toss, what factors would you consider in putting the opposition into bat? 5 points

22. Name three methods of practising batting by yourself. 3 points.

23. Name at least 16 different fielding positions (half point each). 8 points

24. Name two methods of practising bowling by yourself. 2 points

25. If you have the opportunity of selecting a new ball from, say, six different balls, what would you look for in your final selection? 4 points

26. What is a "no ball"? 3 points

27. What are the four main qualities of a captain? 4 points

28. When throwing the ball back to the wicketkeeper, how do you grip the ball and why? 1 point

ANSWERS TO QUESTIONNAIRE:

1. Any six of the following: aim, confidence, making the most of opportunities, fitness, team game, training and practising, listen and learn, watching the great players, read books and watch cricket films, praise and encouragement, play the game hard and to win but within the laws and rules of the game, enjoyment, support the captain and be a good sport and show etiquette (accept decisions, etc.).

2. Any three of the following: watch the ball at all times, count the balls bowled during the over, study the pitch to see how it is playing, talk with your partner who may give you some useful advice, look for field changes. *Always think cricket.* If there is a scoreboard at the ground, look at it and assess the state of the game.

3. Fitness allows you to perform with greater efficiency before the onset of fatigue or tiredness.

4. Any six of the following: alternate arm and leg raises, double back-lifts, press-ups, sit-ups, bending over and touching the toes, rotating the arms, groin exercise, ankle, neck, tuck jumps, sprints, jogging, burpees.

5. A ball will swing in the air if the axis of the ball (seam) is vertical and if one side of the ball is more shiny or smooth than the other side. As the ball travels through the air, the air on the smooth or shiny side is relatively undisturbed. The air flow on the rough side becomes more turbulent. Thus with the differing air flows the ball will swing.

6. I would bowl short of a good length to prevent him from pushing forward.

7. The word "length" means where the ball pitches. The ideal length to bowl is where the batsman hesitates as to whether he should play forward or back. There are five proper lengths to bowl: short of a length, good length, yorker, bouncer and half volley. A full toss, a beamer and a long hop should be avoided at all times.

8. The field set to an in-form batsman to a medium-pace bowler would be defensive, to prevent him from scoring. The bowler's line would be attacking the off stump or slightly outside the off stump to 5/4 off-side field set: e.g., one slip, gully, third man, cover, mid-off, mid-on, mid-wicket, square leg and fine leg.

9. The breeze, the slope of the pitch, and whether one end has more grass than the other.

10. The first two fingers grip down either side of the seam with the angle of the seam pointing towards first slip. The thumb is positioned on the under side of the seam. The ball is gripped loosely and is as far forward in the fingers as possible.

11. He will lose his balance and will fall over, meaning that he is unlikely to bowl the ball consistently straight. He will get no bounce from the pitch and will not be able to bowl as fast or effectively. The front arm should "reach for the sky" and stay up there as long as possible to keep the body upright.

12. Both hands should be together on the bat handle, as high up as possible. With the back of the top hand pointing towards cover, the bottom hand should be gripped loosely.

13. The balance of the bat when picked up, the weight (it is better to have a lighter bat than one that is too heavy for you), a short-handled or long-handled bat, possible additional grips, left or right-handed bat.

14. While using your hands to stop the ball, your body should act as a second line of defence: both feet together forming a 'V', one foot at right angles to the ball, or the barrier style (the front leg forms a barrier with the foot of the other leg also coming into line).

15. You can misfield the ball and give away extra runs, drop a catch in the field or miss a run out chance.
16. He needs to be athletic, agile, decisive, alert, have good equipment, set a good example for a high standard of fielding, liaise with the bowler, be in a relaxed and comfortable position, allow the hands to "give" with the ball when catching, have a high concentration level.
17. "Yes", "No", "Wait".
18. The batsman should back up, turn viewing the ball, note field placings, slide the bat, always run the first run hard.
19. Out, leg bye, bye, wide, no-ball, one short, boundary four, boundary six, cancel previous signal, dead ball.
20. Bowled, caught, run out, hit wicket, handled ball, stumped, obstructing the field, timed out, lbw, hit twice, retired out. He can be out in 10 different ways.
21. Consider the pitch. If it is grassy he will probably bowl because the pitch will suit his seam bowlers; if the weather is overcast the ball will swing and suit his swing bowlers; if the opposition's batting is weak and he has effective fast bowlers; the state of the competition — he may need to bowl a team out twice to win the game to help win that competition.
22. Practising in the garage with the ball in a stocking on a string; practising in front of a mirror; hitting a ball with a wicket against a brick wall. A bat or tennis/rubber ball could also be used.
23. Wicketkeeper, first slip, second slip, third slip, gully, third man, cover, mid-off, mid-on, mid-wicket, square leg, fine leg, leg gully, bat/pad, long-on, long-off, leg slip, extra cover, point, cover point, deep extra cover, deep square leg.
24. Bowling with a ball at one wicket with a marker put down on a good length in a net, or alternatively bowling against a brick wall so that the ball will bounce back and assist you in fielding practice.
25. Dark colour, high seam, oval shaped, and how it fits in the fingers (the feel of it).
26. A no-ball is when a bowler throws the ball; or his front foot or any part thereof does not land behind the bowling crease; or if the back foot cuts the return crease at the point of delivery; or if there are more than two fielders behind square on the leg side.
27. The main qualities of a captain are: he should communicate with his players; he should lead by example; he should outline his strategy for the day's play; any criticism should be constructive and not destructive. He should be knowledgeable on all cricket matters.
28. The ball must be gripped across the seam to prevent it swinging away from its target.